English at Tennessee

English at Tennessee

Tennessee

1794–1988

Kenneth Curry

A Publication of the Department of English
The University of Tennessee, Knoxville, 1989

Published by the Department of English, The University of
Tennessee, Knoxville, with a grant from the Better English Fund,
established by John C. Hodges. Copyright © 1989. All rights re-
served.

Publication Authorization Number: R01-1032-01-001-90

The Department of English
301 McClung Tower
The University of Tennessee
Knoxville, Tennessee 37996-0430

TO
THE MEMORY OF
James Douglas Bruce
John Cunyus Hodges
Alwin Thaler
Roscoe Edward Parker
John Bernard Emperor
PROFESSORS OF ENGLISH

CONTENTS

To the Reader

To the Reader

This account of English Studies and the English Department at the University of Tennessee, Knoxville, is addressed to a small audience: the present members of the English Department, former members of the Department, students who studied English at the University, and to those who received M.A.s and Ph.D.s in the field of English studies.

The narrative reflects the author's own experiences, points of view, and prejudices so that I have not hesitated to use the pronoun "I." In the absence of documentary sources I have used my own recollections and what others-- some of them no longer with us--have told me and which I now recall. I have dedicated the volume to the memory of five Professors of English: James Douglas Bruce, John C. Hodges, Alwin Thaler, Roscoe E. Parker, and John B. Emperor, to whom the present department owes a great debt of gratitude for their example of good scholarship, respect for learning, and to Hodges, Thaler and Parker for establishing the Ph.D. program on a sound foundation. Three of these professors-- Bruce, Hodges, and Emperor--made in their wills substantial bequests of money and books to enable the Department (and the Library) to do important things which the meagre funds allotted to the Department made impossible.

A quick chronological survey of the Department of English indicates that there is an unbroken line of Professors of English who had national--not just local or regional--reputations for their writing and scholarship. The list begins with President Dabney's appointment of Charles W. Kent in 1888 followed by John Bell Henneman, James Douglas Bruce, George Herbert Clarke, John C. Hodges, and Alwin Thaler. And to come to more modern times I think no one would quarrel with my inclusion of the name of the late Professor Richard Beale Davis, whose monumental three-volume Intellectual Life in the Colonial South, 15-85-1763 *(1977) received the National Book Award from the Association of American Publishers in a ceremony at Carnegie Hall in New York. Among those still living or holding positions in the Department I am sure that another name--or two or three-- will come to mind of those who should be included.*

Acknowledgments

I undertook the writing and research for this history of English Studies and the English Department at the invitation of Dr. Joseph B. Trahern, Jr., head of the Department, with the approval of the Department's administrative committee. I am indebted to Dr. Trahern for placing at my disposal materials from his office, and to the able and cheerful secretarial assistance of Mrs. Wanda Giles, Mrs. Sandra Lewis, Mrs. Dinah Brock. I have included information about my sources in the Bibliographical Notes at the end of this study. I wish to thank especially Dr. James R. Montgomery, author of the *Volunteer State Forges Its University* and *Threshold of a New Day*, for placing at my disposal some of his notes which he had collected for these works. Similarly, Mr. Neal O'Steen, who has written several articles on the old days and personalities of the University for the *Tennessee Alumnus*, has provided me with notes that have been helpful to me. Mr. Nick Wyman of Special Collections in the University Library has been helpful in searching for out-of-the-way bits of history in the Archives and for cheerfully bringing up material from the vaults for my use.

My friend and colleague, Bain T. Stewart, formerly head of the Department, has read the chapters of this study as they progressed and has offered suggestions and saved me several times from making factual errors. A few other friends have read parts of the typescript from time to time, but I must not hold them responsible for any mistakes that have crept in or interpretations with which some readers may wish to differ.

Knoxville. November 20, 1987.

Preparation and publication of this volume has been supported by the Better English Fund, established by John C. Hodges.

xi

CHAPTER I

THE BEGINNING TO 1887

The University of Tennessee traces its origin to 1794 when Blount College, named in honor of the state's first governor, was founded. Blount College became East Tennessee College in 1808, then East Tennessee University in 1840, and finally the University of Tennessee in 1879. Throughout its first century the institution suffered from low enrollments and inadequate financial resources. English studies and a formally organized English Department did not exist in nineteenth-century colleges, but some study of what were later designated as English studies did take place. At all colleges in the pre-Civil War South training in English composition and the study of English critical style and literature were a digression and, when listed in catalogs, would be called rhetoric and belles-lettres. The college curriculum was limited. During the first two years the classics (Latin and Greek) and mathematics were the required staple, with some physical or natural science taught in the third. In the fourth year the professor of moral philosophy, often the president, might include literature in his lectures. Blair's <u>Rhetoric</u> and Kames' <u>Elements of Criticism</u> are often cited as texts. Records of the early years at Blount College and East Tennessee College are scanty, but a file of college catalogs from 1838 forward lets us learn something about English studies during those years, which followed in general the practices of other colleges. The catalog for 1839 states that "A Weekly Exercise in Composition and Declamation" was required during the Freshman year. During the Sophomore and Junior years the requirement was for "Weekly Rhetorical Exercises, Composition, Declamation or Debates." For the Senior year these requirements continued: "A stated Rhetorical Exercise, Compositions, Original Declamations or Forensic Discussions." Juniors and Seniors also had the privilege of listening to eleven lectures, number eleven of which was "Belles-Lettres." We are not told how these requirements were met, but informal arrangements would have been necessary since the number both of faculty and students was too small for many formally organized arrangements. Enrollments during most of the first century were about one hundred. In 1847–48 the numbers peaked at 140, but in 1851–52 had sunk to a low of 66!

During its first century the University had a preparatory department which accounted for one half or more of the enrollment. The faculty seldom numbered more than four with the president sharing in the teaching of courses. The teaching load varied from twenty-four to twenty-seven hours. Many tutors and professors were clergymen who may have preached on Sundays in local pulpits to supplement their meager salaries. A few professors and presidents had relatively long tenures, but few stayed more than three or four years before moving on to other careers or to more affluent institutions. President Estabrook served from 1834 to 1850 when he resigned in discouragement to manage his farm in Anderson County; President Humes served from 1866 to 1883; Professor Richard Llewellyn Kirkpatrick, a graduate of the class of 1845, served in sequence as professor of Greek and Latin, mathematics, English, and finally of history until his death in 1879. The modern idea of professional specialization together with a lifetime commitment to teaching, study, and research at one institution was yet to come.

But to return to the curriculum. The catalog of 1843–44 is more specific about requirements in composition and public speaking. Freshmen presented written translations or English compositions and declaimed every two weeks before a class and twice a session before the college. The annual commencement exercises emphasized student speeches, and the best speakers received prizes.

The two literary societies, Chi Delta and Philomathesian, provided an extra-curricular activity for students interested in writing and speaking. The societies had weekly meetings in their own rooms, had their own libraries of 500 or 600 volumes, and offered declamations or debates at their meetings. At least once a year the societies held a public debate. William Gibbs McAdoo, Jr., gives a lively account of one such debate. In 1880 McAdoo and his cousin, Charles Humes (a nephew of President Humes), as members of the Chi Delta Society, debated on the subject of the Mormons, took the less popular side, and according to the decision of the five judges won the debate. Staub's Theatre, newly built in downtown Knoxville, seated 1,500 and was filled to overflowing for the event. Certainly taste in public entertainment has changed in a century. Skill in the writing and delivery of declamations was highly valued and a necessary part of the education of young men who aspired to fame in the pulpit, at the bar, or in the political forum-- the destination of many of the University's graduates.

In the early 1840s some University seniors assisted by the faculty produced a monthly magazine between 1841 and 1843 entitled the University Magazine, and now preserved in two volumes of three hundred pages each. In addition to a few short stories or sketches and poems, there are several essays on such contemporary writers as William Cullen Bryant, Oliver W. Holmes, Lydia Sigourney, Felicia Hemans, and Washington Irving. Samuel Bugg, a senior, contributed an essay on Byron's English Bards originally written "to discharge a duty connected with our collegiate exercises." Essays upon current topics were Senior J. H. Martin's "The Predicted Dissolution of the Union," for which he held "awesome fears," a debate on the two sides of capital punishment, "The Importance of Female Education," and an essay of local interest, "Education in East Tennessee," which deplored the large number of small sectarian colleges. J. H. Martin, who once owned the second volume, has annotated several essays to indicate the authors' names. Martin seems to have been the editor assisted by Samuel Bugg and J. B. Cooke. Horace Maynard, a member of the faculty since 1838, William J. Keith, the professor of classics, and Thomas Humes, later president of the University were non-student contributors as well as President Estabrook, whose baccalaureate address was reprinted. The evidence of these two volumes points to a lively interest in the issues of the day and contemporary literature. These young writers and their literary advisers have nothing of which to be ashamed. These two volumes reveal a high standard of literary competence, a sensitivity to literature, and concern for the problems that were soon to overwhelm the South, the nation, and their own personal lives.

Commencements in these early days were the showcases for graduates and students to display their skills in oratory and forensics. Many programs of these commencements survive, and the one for August 5, 1843 is representative, and reveals a strong accent on literature.

John B. Brooks, one of the graduates, spoke on "The Dramatic Writings of Shakespeare," while Samuel Bugg and Dawson A. Walker, another graduate, led a discussion on the question: "Have the Writings of Sir Walter Scott exerted a beneficial effect upon English Literature?" In addition, sixteen orations, discussions, eulogies, or colloquies were offered up on that hot August day. One wonders how many of the audience endured to the end!

The resignation of a discouraged President Estabrook in 1850, after sixteen years of service, brought the University to another crisis. The next decade was marked by dropping enrollments, the closing of the University during the fall of 1853 and for the spring of 1858 as four presidents struggled to keep open the doors of the institution: William B. Reese (1850-53), The Rev. George Cooke (1853-1857); The Rev. William D. Carnes (1858-60), who had served earlier as professor of ancient languages and belles-lettres and principal of the preparatory department; The Rev. J. J. Ridley (1860- February 1862) during whose term the war brought the closing of the University.

When the University reopened after the Civil War its buildings and grounds were in ruins and its faculty dispersed so that only a preparatory department would open to receive twenty students in rooms of the Deaf and Dumb Asylum in downtown Knoxville. It was not until 1871 that the University had a graduating class, a decade after the war began.

Although the new president, The Rev. Thomas W. Humes, rector of St. John's Episcopal Church, represented the traditional classical curriculum, the curriculum was expanding to include agriculture and mechanics. This turn away from emphasis upon Latin and Greek in favor of study of English and modern languages is further evidenced by the appointment of the first professor of English in 1867: The Rev. Francis Michael Grace, a graduate of the class of 1849, and a Methodist minister from Alabama. Grace remained until 1870 when he left for Hiawassee College, where he became president. His place was filled by Richard Llewellyn Kirkpatrick, M.A., 1845, who had been professor of the Latin language and literature. By 1870 enrollment reached 183, but only 35 were in the college so that

collegiate work in English was necessarily on an elementary
and restricted level.

In 1878 Edward S. Joynes (M.A. Virginia) joined the
faculty as Professor of English Language and Belles-
Lettres, coming from Vanderbilt, where he had been one of
the original professors, but a charge of drinking leveled
against him led to his dismissal and his coming to the more
liberal and worldly atmosphere of the University of East
Tennessee. Joynes proved to be a lively addition to the
staff.

Philander P. Claxton, a student during Joynes' tenure
at the University remembers him thus: "He wore a Prince
Albert coat with a white cravat and carried a gold headed
walking stick which he liked to twirl as he walked."
Claxton calls him an excellent scholar and good teacher.
Claxton describes the study of English as emphasizing
language with illustrative selections and pointing out
there were no courses in English or American literature.
Joynes left in 1882 for the University of South Carolina
where he had a distinguished career as professor of modern
languages and author of several textbooks in that field.

In 1877 William Gibbs McAdoo, Sr., returned to
Knoxville and the University, not as a professor but as an
instructor of English in the preparatory department.
McAdoo's diaries, which he kept for over forty years,
provide fascinating glimpses into those bleak years before
and after the Civil War. A Confederate sympathizer, McAdoo
in 1862 had moved from Knoxville to Georgia to look after
family property belonging to his wife, but the aftermath of
the war left the family impoverished. After failing to win
an election to a judgeship (he was a lawyer by profession)
he sought to return to his native East Tennessee. The
appointment of his nephew, Dr. William Morrow, to the board
of trustees assured his selection as an instructor at the
salary of $1,500.00 per year. For nine years McAdoo
struggled to teach bored and uninterested students and in
his diaries recorded his frustrations and the petty
jealousies among the faculty. He described the students as
"wonderfully dull" and intended "to have some of them
dismissed for incapacity." In 1879 McAdoo became librarian
(that post was usually held as a part-time job by a
professor) as well as an instructor, and reported that the

library had 3,326 volumes. A strict disciplinarian (McAdoo had been a captain of a company of East Tennesseans during the Mexican War), he opposed the lenient and "modern" attitude of the young Joynes and resisted the suggestion of an honor system. Faculty meetings irritated him. President Humes was too lenient a presiding officer and some professors--Joynes in particular--delighted to hear themselves talk. Professor Brown was a "contentious and bigoted fool." The McAdoos were prolific writers (she wrote novels) and McAdoo's sonnets appeared in the Knoxville newspaper, but his nephew thought publication of poetry by a college professor to be undignified. In January 1885 McAdoo was finally made an adjunct professor of English and remained in this post a year when his appointment was not renewed at the election of the faculty in June 1886. The University's Chi Delta Crescent deplored the departure of one who had "grown gray" in the service of the University. As a financial footnote the loss of this position left McAdoo with his Mexican War pension of $8.00 per month as his principal income. His diaries and other contemporary reminiscences give little information about his classes or the student response to his tuition, but his son wrote this tribute of his father: "My father had a fine sense of precision and form. His hobbies and pursuits were all intellectual; I remember clearly his deep interest in literature, and in such amiable sciences as botany, astronomy, and geology. He liked poetry, to read it and to write it, and he had a ready facility in the use of poetic forms, especially in the composition of sonnets." It is difficult to believe that a man with such wide literary culture and personal skill in composition did not impart some of that love, enthusiasm, and skill in reading and writing to a few of his more perceptive students.

Rodes Massie (M.A., D.L. Virginia) replaced Edward Joynes in 1882 as Professor of English and Modern Languages. In 1883 after the trustees fired President Humes, Massie served for two years as chairman of the faculty during the four-year interregnum between Presidents Hume and Dabney. He presided at board meetings, conferred degrees at commencement, and acted as executive head. In 1888, however, the new president, Charles W. Dabney, Jr., fired Massie and retained only two of the old faculty. And so Massie disappears from the scene at Tennessee.

In 1886 and 1887, during the years the University had no president, two Ph.D.s were awarded to two brothers: William Isaac Thomas and Price Thomas. Price Thomas was in the scientific curriculum, and W. I. Thomas in the classical. The catalogs do not state the requirements for these advanced degrees, and no dissertations, if written, survive. W. I. Thomas was successively instructor in modern languages and natural history, the ancient and modern languages, and finally an adjunct professor of English and modern language as well as librarian. Thomas left the University in 1888 for a year of graduate study in Germany, and he returned not to the University but to Oberlin College where he became professor of English. Thomas, when still at Oberlin, moved to the study of sociology, took a Ph.D. in sociology at the University of Chicago, where he became a professor of sociology and had a distinguished career as a writer in that field. The entries in Who Was Who do not mention this doctoral degree from Tennessee. Perhaps he could be claimed as the first Ph.D. in English, but I find no evidence to support the claim.

One of the two professors Dabney chose to retain was Thomas C. Karns, an alumnus of the University, who served in various roles from 1886 to 1899. He was Associate Professor of the English Language and Literature in 1888-89, had served as head of the preparatory department in its last days, later became Associate Professor of history and Philosophy, librarian, and helped to train students who planned to be teachers.

The presidency of the young, energetic Dabney, with his Ph.D. from Göttingen in chemistry and mineralogy, was to introduce needed changes in the old way of doing things and to make the University of Tennessee a modern university where faculty appointments would be based on scholastic qualifications and degrees from prestigious universities and not upon kinship to a trustee or influential politician.

Notes

*I have omitted most details of the history of the
University since that material can be readily found in J.
R. Montgomery's, S. J. Folmsbee's and L. S. Greene's To
Foster Knowledge (1984), the lengthiest study. Some earlier
histories, however, present a livelier picture of the
University's history: J. R. Montgomery's The Volunteer
State Forges Its University 1887-1919 (1966) and Threshold
of a New Day 1919-1946 (1971).   Neal O'Steen's Tennessee
Partners (1986), a history of the Alumni Association, and
his articles in The Tennessee Alumnus (especially those on
the McAdoos) bring to life events and personalities of the
past.*

*An article by Dr. John Bell Henneman, Professor of
English at the University (1893-1900), "The Study of English
in the South," in the Sewanee Review, II, 1893-94, provides
an excellent survey of the collegiate studies in English in
the antebellum South. Since the University of Tennessee did
not differ from other colleges in the South this article by
one of its own professors has been most helpful in writing
this first chapter.*

*Neal O'Steen's biographical articles on McAdoo and
Joynes in the Tennessee Alumnus (Fall, 1984, and Spring,
1983) give further details about these colorful professors
of the 1870s and 1880s. Joynes, a powerful personality
during his tenure (1878-82) at the University, became an
advisor to Judge Oliver P. Temple, leader of the Board of
Trustees, and continued to write and advise him about
University matters long after he had moved to South
Carolina. "Disturbed and depressing conditions at the
University of Tennessee" had persuaded him to accept the
offer from South Carolina, a year before the ouster of
President Humes in 1883.*

CHAPTER II

ENGLISH UNDER THE DABNEY ADMINISTRATION

Dabney's administration brought the University into the modern world. The four presidentless years from 1883 to 1887 marked one of the most dismal periods in the history of the University, and the trustees willingly gave the new president authority to bring about needed changes. A measure of his success can be seen in the numbers. In 1887 enrollment was only 174, but by the end of his administration in 1904 it reached 800. At thirty-two Charles W. Dabney, Jr. was young, energetic, well-educated, and with his Ph.D. in chemistry and mineralogy from Göttingen. Within his first few years Dabney made four sweeping changes: elimination of the preparatory department and military discipline for the students (now called students and not cadets), adoption of standards of admission, and opening the doors of the University to women in 1893. The admission of women in 1893 brought not only a stimulus to the enrollments but a new element of competition in the classroom as the women quickly proved their ability to compete with the men. The faculty awarded a tuition scholarship to the student with the highest grade average at the end of the freshman, sophomore, and junior year. The women won all three of these scholarships the first year! More important than these changes, however, was Dabney's policy of bringing in young, academically qualified men to fill the various professorships even though he had been forced to effect this change by firing all but two of the old faculty.

President Dabney and the trustees were committed to expanding the programs of the University to include agriculture and the mechanic arts as indeed the Morrill Act of 1862 had mandated for land-grant institutions. A year after Dabney's arrival the administration of the University and its programs of instruction began to look recognizably like those of later years. The faculty were divided into ten schools of which the School of English and Modern Language was one (containing three faculty members). These ten schools--later they would be called departments--were organized under the College of Agriculture, Mechanic Arts and Sciences. The other two units of the University were

[9]

the Graduate School (existing largely on paper) and the
Medical Units then at Nashville. Although the words
classical and liberal arts did not appear in the new
catalog, most of the subjects in this new arrangement were
adopted from the old classical curriculum.

The reorganization of the University into ten schools
(the later departments) resulted in the increasing ability
of the departments to make recommendations affecting their
welfare. This sentence from the catalog of 1889-90 is
important: "The Professors, Associate Professors and
Instructors in each School constitute a Standing Committee,
to which are referred questions relating to the School under
their control, but their action is subject to the approval
of the General Faculty." It was several decades before the
presidents shared much of their power to make appointments
and to approve promotions and raises. Even today the
recommendations of the Department do not always survive a
review by a complex hierarchy of officials above the
departmental level. But an important beginning of shared
responsibility in governance had been made.

Dabney's first appointment of an English professor was
a wise one. Charles W. Kent (1860-1917), an M.A. from the
University of Virginia and a Ph.D. from Leipzig, had also
studied at Dabney's old University (Göttingen) and Berlin.
Only twenty-eight when he assumed his duties, Kent
inaugurated the tradition of scholarly publishing by
professors in the Department, and in 1889 published an
edition of the Old English poem Elene complete with
introduction, text, notes, and vocabulary. With Charles W.
Kent the professors of English begin to emerge as distinct
personalities. President Hoskins, who had planned to write
a history of the University wrote some recollections of
Kent, Bruce, and Burke (this three-page sketch is among the
Hoskins papers in the Special Collections Room). Hoskins
had been one of Kent's students and writes of him thus: "It
was my pleasure and privilege to study under Dr. Kent. He
was one of the most inspiring and delightful lecturers in
the classroom. He was a man of fine personality and great
enthusiasm. He inspired his students with a love for
literature. He was an outstanding public speaker and was
called upon to lecture at various institutions of learning."
Hoskins failed to mention that Kent was a classmate of

Woodrow Wilson at the University of Virginia and belonged to the inner circle of Wilson's college friends. Kent and Wilson maintained a regular if infrequent correspondence, and Wilson often refers to Kent as "Charley" in letters to other friends. The highlight for the University of Kent's friendship with Wilson came in 1890 when Kent secured Wilson as the commencement speaker. Wilson, already a professor at Princeton and a rising star noted for his eloquence, held the attention of an audience of about a thousand at Staub's Opera House with his speech "Leaders of Men." Five years after Kent arrived on the campus, his old school, the University of Virginia, offered him in 1893 a newly endowed chair, which he accepted and where he remained for the rest of his life. He later published editions of Tennyson and Poe and was one of the editors of the fifteen-volume Library of Southern Literature.

The catalog of 1889-90 listed all English courses on one page. These brief descriptions reveal that history was taught as part of the English curriculum. The Sub-Freshman Class had not only grammar and syntax but history of the United States and General History. We are told that in the Freshman Class theory and practice of composition were taught by the study of good models, by frequent written exercises, accompanied by the study of the history of England with Montgomery's history as text. The Sophomore Class studied the history of the English language, Anglo-Saxon, and word analysis. Texts were Lounsbury's History of the English Language, Corson's Saxon and Early English, Haldeman's Outline of Etymology, and Chaucer's poems. The Junior Class studied English literature, qualities of style, critical essays, and versification. Among the texts was G. L. Craik's The English of Shakespeare, illustrated in a philological commentary on Julius Caesar, ed. by W. J. Rolfe, 1888. The Senior Class studied the history of civilization and constitutional history--no mention of literature. This outline, bare as it is, tells us a good deal. Skill and practice in composition were emphasized, but the study of literature stressed its philological rather than literary content. This emphasis seems to reflect the training of Kent in philology and in the earlier periods of English literature.

Dabney chose as Kent's successor Thomas Bell Henneman

(1864-1908), an M.A. from the University of Virginia and a
Ph.D. from the University of Berlin. Henneman was twenty-
nine when he came to the University and continued Dabney's
policy of bringing in young men imbued with the new spirit
of scholarship and research that was transforming American
higher education. Henneman remained at the University for
seven years (1893-1900) until he left for the University of
the South, where he succeeded his friend, William P. Trent,
not only as professor of English but as editor of the
Sewanee Review. Henneman later became dean at the
University of the South. A prolific writer, Henneman
contributed one or more essays and book reviews to the
Sewanee Review every year from 1892 (the first volume) until
1908. A glance at some of these essays reveals that the
author was a man of broad intellectual and literary
interests who possessed the ability to express his thoughts
clearly, succinctly, and gracefully. His article (written
while he was a professor at the University) in the second
volume, "The Study of English in the South," can be highly
recommended to any one seeking a view of higher education in
Southern colleges as it concerned English studies. "The
Modern Spirit in Literature," "Dryden After Two Centuries,"
"The Man Shakespeare: His Growth as an Artist," and "The
Bronte Sisters" show a wide range of interest.

As the professor of English Henneman influenced changes
in the English curriculum as the catalog of 1899-1900 will
show. Henneman turned away from the stress upon
philological study and medieval literature and Old English
towards American literature, Romantic poetry, and
nineteenth-century prose and poetry. In the fall Freshman
English was devoted to the writing of themes; in the winter
themes on literature were accompanied by a survey of the
history of English literature and lectures on English
history; in the spring themes continued to be written twice
a week with lectures on the development of the English
language. In the fall Sophomore English continued the
writing of themes; in the winter prose masterpieces and
lyric forms of verse were read; and in the spring topics in
American literature from poetry, fiction, essays, history
and biography were introduced. Junior English had
nineteenth-century prose, Romantic poetry, and Victorian
poetry. The Senior year was devoted to the early drama and

the plays of Shakespeare. A parallel course in English philology provided a year's work in Old English prose and poetry for those who wished that option. The catalog lists many graduate courses in every subject from Old English to Browning, but since there were never more than one or two graduate students I wonder who would enroll in these courses and how a faculty consisting of only two persons could teach all these courses. The catalog, incidentally, lists the times at which the courses for the four undergraduate years met, and the interested reader may read with alarm that classes on Saturday prevailed even into the afternoon!

In 1894 The Dial published a series of articles on English studies in American colleges, and Henneman wrote a letter to the editor published in the issue for December 16, 1894 detailing the program at the University of Tennessee:

> We have made the serious study of American literary conditions the subject for investigation for one whole year, just because it contains the essence of our nationality and brings the facts and possibilities of American life and authorship closer home to the youthful aspirant. Similarly, the study of the nineteenth century English writers, both in prose and in verse, best bears the impress of the modern consciousness and reproduces most clearly existing tendencies and habits of thought. The prolonged study of Shakespeare by the maturest students is a just recognition of the poet's supreme power.

Henneman also stressed in his letter that all work in English was centered in the library, "the workshop of the English classes."

We do not have any testimonials from Henneman's students at the University, but two students at the University of the South spoke highly of Henneman. Thomas Ewing Dabney, a newspaper editor in New Mexico who took an M.A. at Harvard, wrote: "I took courses under, among others, George Lyman Kittredge. I felt that Harvard at that time had no one in literature superior to Sewanee's John Bell Henneman, either as scholar or inspiring teacher." Eleanor W. Thomas, the first woman student at Sewanee and later head of the English department at Western Reserve, wrote in 1954: "I never had more thorough teaching than from Professor John Bell Henneman." All evidence points to Henneman as an able and dynamic professor.

A measure of the atmosphere of a college is to be found in its student publications. The two volumes of The University of Tennessee Magazine for 1894 and 1895, edited and written by students, speak well of their abilities. Although no contributor ever achieved great fame, Norman H. Pitman, 1895, later wrote fiction and essays based upon his later experiences in China and enjoyed a modest literary reputation. Edwin M. Wiley, another editor and contributor, had a career in librarianship at Tennessee, Vanderbilt, Stanford, the Library of Congress, and wrote professional articles. The students showed their interest in the history of the University by short articles on former presidents Estabrook, Coffin, and Reese; by Wiley's article on University alumni in Knoxville; and by a short article on the English Department. The article does not mention Dr. Henneman or Mr. Black, who constituted the English faculty, but this account closely parallels the letter, already cited, which Henneman addressed to the editor of The Dial. The poems and stories are conventional and of no great originality, and the topics chosen for essays show the authors and works these students knew and, by inference, had studied in class: Shakespeare (Lear, Taming of the Shrew), Goldsmith, Scott, Austen, and such contemporary authors as Howells and James. An account, however, of the controversial Yellow Book shows that the campus literati were not attuned to the fashionable decadence provided by that magazine of art and letters. The drawings of Beardsley, Steer, and Beerbohm were disparaged, and the writings were dismissed because there is "nothing in it to uplift." Although The University of Tennessee Magazine will disappoint a reader looking for evidence of genius, the volumes show that the writing and study of literature were congenial to the students under the care of Professor Henneman.

1899 saw the appointment of the first woman to the faculty. Florence Skeffington, an M.A. from Mary Sharp College, was appointed an instructor of English, promoted to

Assistant Professor, and later to Dean of Women. Miss Skeffington stayed until 1905, and one of her students, Benton White, has left this lively sketch:

> Miss Skeffington taught Freshman English, and introduced us to the doubtful joy of writing themes. These she corrected copiously in an angular, flowing, and almost illegible hand, using the brightest of red ink. This was the basis for a skit in one of the annuals. It was supposed to be a "Jack" for the interpretation of Miss Skeffington's criticism of freshman themes. For the benefit of the uninitiated, a "Jack" was an English translation of certain Latin classics authored by Caesar, Virgil, and Cicero . . . a handy thing to have around, but frowned on by the faculty. She was a hard worker, a person not easily dismayed by what she read; a good and enthusiastic teacher.
>
> The English faculty during these years was normally no more than two: the Professor of English, who had a Ph.D., and an instructor who had usually just received an M.A. from the University. One exception was Associate Professor Thomas C. Karns, who was in charge of the fledgling program in teacher training and of a four-year program that attempted to offer an inter-disciplinary major with an emphasis upon writing, literature, history, political science, psychology, and logic. Karns's duties also involved visiting schools in the state. How Professor Karns taught his classes, traveled, and made public speeches is difficult to conceive. The various instructors and assistant professors who assisted the professor certainly devoted their talents to Freshman English. But some of those who taught for only a year or two had subsequent careers of some renown. Kenneth Matheson became president of Drexel Institute, Norman H. Pitman, a writer of fiction and essays based upon his later experiences in China; Edwin M. Wiley, a respected University librarian; Joseph Black, a Knoxville lawyer; William Isaac Thomas, a distinguished sociologist at the University of Chicago; and Emilie W. McVea,

president of Sweet Briar College.

The spirit of a time and place is hard to realize after the passing of almost a century. But I have concluded that the years of Dabney's administration brought new life and energy to a moribund institution. After Dabney's arrival in 1887 he wrote his wife that the faculty was "composed of some young fellows mostly from around here, decent enough, but ordinary." When he had finished his new hiring he had doubled the size of the faculty, increased enrollments, introduced new courses in science, agriculture, and engineering, and ended the old days when the faculty was recruited from decent but ordinary young men (usually related to trustees and influential citizens). Despite the low pay and heavy teaching loads the morale of the faculty and students appears to have been high. Dean Thomas Jordan reflected in 1911: "There was a spirit of oneness in ideals and harmony of intercourse" within the school.

The departure of Henneman in 1900 enabled Dabney to make a third appointment to the chair of English, and again he chose a Virginian, with training at a German University, and with a Ph.D. from Johns Hopkins. At thirty-eight James Douglas Bruce was a decade older than Kent and Henneman at the time of their appointments, but he came with experience as a professor at Bryn Mawr and several substantial articles in scholarly journals to his credit. To Dabney then the Department of English owes a debt of gratitude for three first-class appointments and for helping to establish a tradition where respect for learning and a search for distinction became an accepted way of life.

Since Dabney left in 1904 for his new post as President of the University of Cincinnati an account of the newly appointed Bruce and his era belongs to the next chapter of this history: English Under the Ayres Administration.

Notes

The catalogs of bygone years can often mislead. For instance, the catalog for 1888-89 lists Professor Norwood as the Professor of the newly created School of English and Modern Languages. Dabney had employed Thomas L. Norwood, an M.A. from North Carolina, as successor to the fired Rodes Massie as professor of English and as Dean of the University, a new position which he had created to relieve himself of some of the growing duties of administration. But Norwood died during the spring or summer of 1888--after the catalog had been printed. Charles W. Kent took his place as Professor of English, and the post of Dean by Thomas W. Jordan, who was also Professor of Latin. My reading of old catalogs arouses a persistent suspicion that many courses were seldom if ever given when the smallness of the staff and the correspondingly small numbers of students are considered. An excellent source of information about John B. Henneman is the file of the Sewanee Review during the years of his editorship and especially the issue following his death in 1908 which contains tributes from several persons and Dr. Dubose's speech at a memorial service. The quotations from the reminiscences of his Sewanee students are from Arthur B. Chitty, A Sewanee Sampler, Sewanee University Press, 1978.

The Virginia Connection

As I gathered biographical details about the professors who came to the University during and just before the Dabney era I could not ignore the Virginia connection. Dabney, A Virginian and graduate of Hampden-Sydney College, had attended the University of Virginia for graduate study before going to Germany for his Ph.D. His first appointment to the English faculty was Dr. Charles W. Kent, a graduate of the University of Virginia and a Ph.D. from Leipzig, even though in hiring him Dabney had to fire Rodes Massie, a Virginia M.A., who had also followed a Virginia alumnus, Edward S. Joynes (1878-82). When Kent was called back to the University of Virginia to fill a newly endowed chair, Dabney then employed Dr. John Bell Henneman, a South Carolinian, but a graduate of Virginia with a Ph.D. from Berlin. When Henneman went to the University of the South in 1900 he was succeeded by Dr. James Douglas Bruce, another Virginian and graduate of the University of Virginia. He later studied in Germany at Dabney's old University, Göttingen, but had a Ph.D. from Johns Hopkins, newly established in Baltimore on the model of the German University. But this is not quite the end of the Virginia connection. When Henneman went to Sewanee he took the place vacated by William P. Trent, another graduate of Virginia, who was on his way to Columbia University. All these men were friends and contemporaries of each other-- or at least known to each other--at the University of Virginia. In 1913 Dr. Bruce, who wished to help his student, Joseph W. Krutch, wrote to his old Virginia friend, William P. Trent, to secure a scholarship for Krutch at Columbia. The influence of the University of Virginia upon English studies in the South is recorded in Henneman's article in the second volume of the Sewanee Review, where all the names I have cited can be found.

The death of Bruce in 1923 broke the chain which had been unbroken for forty-five years. In the 1940s the coming of Dr. F. DeWolfe Miller and Dr. Richard Beale Davis revived briefly the Virginia connection.

CHAPTER III

ENGLISH UNDER PRESIDENT AYRES
AND JAMES DOUGLAS BRUCE

The administration of Brown Ayres (1904-1919) continued the policies of President Dabney. Ayres was committed to strengthening and extending the growth of programs in agriculture and engineering, to extending the influence of the University throughout the state, and to securing adequate financial support for the University from the legislature. Ayres, a Memphian, had studied engineering at Washington and Lee and graduated from Stevens Institute of Technology. He did graduate work at Johns Hopkins, then served as professor of physics and engineering at Tulane University, and later became dean and acting president of that institution. Edwin Mims in his article on Ayres in the Dictionary of American Biography gives Ayres the credit for "outlining the plans and seeing the vision" for reorganizing the University. "He appealed to reasonable men," as Mims phrased it, "by his scientific method, practical sense, and zeal for higher education." Ayres, with the assistance of several trustees and the sure political instincts of Harcourt A. Morgan, dean of the College of Agriculture, secured the first annual appropriations from the legislature to the University. Ayres Hall, built with the proceeds from the first adequate appropriation from the state, stands today as a fitting memorial to Ayres' pioneering success.

Ayres reorganized the University into the separate colleges and departments with which we are familiar: the College of Liberal Arts, the College of Agriculture, the College of Engineering, with separate departments of law and education, later to become separate colleges. Ayres spent much of his time traveling throughout the state promoting a favorable image for the institution and in lobbying the legislature for funds. The deans tended to most of the day-to-day routine of running the University and looked after the steadily increasing numbers of students.

The English Department, if we may use that impressive title to describe an entity consisting of only Professor J. Douglas Bruce and Assistant Professor Florence Skeffington,

[19]

was left free to organize its own courses. It is worth
noting how the courses change with the coming and going of
the holder of the chair. Dr. Kent, after his arrival in
1888, stressed philology, Old English, medieval English,
Chaucer, and Shakespeare. Dr. Henneman, after his arrival
in 1893, modified the emphasis upon the older period and
offered options. A two-year program in philology was
parallel to the literary courses, and a course in the
English novel alternated with junior and senior courses in
medieval and Renaissance literature. When Bruce arrived in
1900, he swept away all options including the introduction
of American literature into the Sophomore English course,
then a requirement for all students. The year-long course
was devoted to English poetry with Ward's English Poets as
the text. The Junior year had two quarters of Romantic
poetry and one of Victorian: the Senior year, two quarters
of Shakespeare and one of Chaucer's Canterbury Tales. The
graduate course was a year's study of Anglo-Saxon. The one
course in English that seems never to change is Freshman
English. The parallel readings in class may change from
models of good prose to readings in English history, but the
emphasis is always upon the writing of themes, themes, and
more themes! Since two persons provided all the instruction
during the early years of the Bruce period, the offerings
had to reflect the tastes and specialties of the senior
professor. Bruce's emphasis upon poetry is worth noticing,
whereas Henneman, with his skill and productivity in the
writing of essays, had included more prose.

Miss Emilie Watts McVea (1867-1928), although not
listed as a member of the English Department, taught courses
in English (1902-1904) in the Department of Education. Dr.
Philander P. Claxton became head of this new department in
the early 1900s. With Miss Skeffington, Miss McVea taught a
course in the theory of teaching English courses in
secondary schools. The department of education had a two-
year course in the great world classics, very similar to the
courses now offered in the English Department, and open to
sophomores and juniors. Miss McVea left the University to
become dean of women at the University of Cincinnati, where
Dabney was president, and from Cincinnati went on to be
president of Sweet Briar College. After her retirement from
Sweet Briar Miss McVea taught English at Rollins College,

where she was a popular lecturer and public speaker in Winter Park and Orlando. Incidentally, these courses in English are not listed in the catalog after the departure of Miss Skeffington and Miss McVea.

James Douglas Bruce (1862-1923) is a professor to whom the present Department and the University owe a great debt of gratitude. A Virginia aristocrat, born on a large plantation into one of the First Families of Virginia, he commanded awe and respect, if not always affection. Benton White, whose recollection of Miss Skeffington has been quoted, also left a description of Dr. Bruce from whom he had Sophomore English. White's remarks should be read with the caveat that he was more interested in mathematics, football, college pranks, and college activities than in English.

Dr. Bruce, "universally called 'old J Doug', taught the higher branches of English literature . . . specifically four volumes of 'Wards English Poets.' Who will ever forget them--or him? He doubtless knew his subject right down to the ground; but he hated what he was doing; disliked his students, who disliked him; and Mr. Wards poets were caught in the middle. There was one thing he could do, tho . . . he could read poetry -- and how he could read it!

He could take some such poem as Beowulf written in Anglo Saxon (a language dead as Sanskrit), and as he read it you could hear the clang of battle axe on shield, the whistle of arrows; the slither of sword on sword; the shouts of the victors; the groans of the wounded. A fidgety, uninterested and hostile class would sit motionless and almost breathless while he read. But it was all too seldom that he did any such things. And I would class him as the poorest teacher I ever studied under.

If student evaluations of the faculty had been dreamed of in those days, it is plain that Bruce would have been unfavorably rated, and if such ratings were taken seriously

as to retention of professors, the University would have
lost one of its few distinguished professors and even fewer
generous benefactors. Am I arguing against taking seriously
student evaluations?

Joseph Wood Krutch, a student of Bruce some ten years
after White, has left another reminiscence in his
autobiography, <u>More Lives Than One</u>. Krutch also remembers
Bruce's impatience and boredom with students, but concedes
that "he was ready to respond to any flicker of interest on
the part of a student, but he had so long ago given up hope
of finding any member of the class who regarded a course in
English Literature as more than a conventional routine which
it was necessary to go through that he used to announce
before examination time: 'When I ask you a question I want
you to tell me exactly what I have told you. I am not
interested in your opinions because I do not think they are
of any value!'" An important advantage Krutch derived from
his study with Bruce was Bruce's recommendation of him to
his life-long friend and fellow Virginian, William P. Trent,
a professor of English at Columbia University, who later
directed Krutch's thesis. Krutch remembered the three
courses with Bruce--Romantic poets, Chaucer, and
Shakespeare--as opening new worlds. "I can still repeat
passages from Shelley and Keats which I then committed to
memory."

Other students, however, have been more complimentary
about Bruce's teaching than White and Krutch. Mrs. Dorothy
Greve McAllester spoke approvingly of Bruce as a challenging
teacher. Mr. James P. Hess, business manager of the
University and secretary to the Board of Trustees, had been
a student and an assistant to Bruce, and he often spoke to
me highly of Bruce whom he greatly admired as teacher,
friend, and scholar. John Thornburgh, a Knoxville lawyer
and judge, praised Bruce's teaching and credited him with
having instilled in him a life-long love of Shakespeare.
Bain Stewart recalls vividly a conversation which he had
with an alumnus from those early days who spoke at length of
Bruce and his admiration for him. Miss Eleanor Burke
remembered Dr. Bruce as a delightful person and one with a
fund of good stories and the latest news.

President Hoskins, although not a student of Bruce, was
the Professor of History and Dean of the College of Liberal

Arts during Bruce's tenure at the University, and has written of him in a short sketch probably intended for his uncompleted history of the University. He wrote of Bruce as "rigid and exacting in his requirements" but still inspiring his students with a love of literature, especially poetry. "In my travels around the State," Hoskins remembers, "more of the former students spoke in high terms of Dr. Bruce than perhaps of any other man. While they were studying under him they did not particularly like him but they had great respect for his scholarship and thoroughness and said they benefitted under him more than any other teacher." Hoskins greatly admired Bruce and appreciated his services to the University.

Bruce's specialty was Arthurian literature, and his two-volume magnum opus appeared in 1923: Evolution of Arthurian Romance from the beginnings down to the year 1300 (Baltimore: John Hopkins Press). This work had been anticipated by several long articles in Modern Philology, Modern Language Notes, and PMLA. Bruce also published lighter ("middle-brow") essays on the novelists Balzac, Thackeray, and Disraeli in the Sewanee Review, then edited by J. B. Henneman. His stature as a scholar was recognized in 1918 by his election to the presidency of the Modern Language Association of America.

Perhaps the greatest claim Bruce makes to the gratitude of the University was the gift of his splendid library of 6,500 books. The collection was a remarkable one in its quality and monetary value: long runs of scholarly journals and publications of antiquarian and historical societies, editions of standards authors, and individual volumes of biography and criticism indispensable to a scholar and teacher in his day-to-day work. Bruce's scholarship required a library of this character and specialization, and since the library had meager resources, he purchased what he needed from his own funds. Happily his private income enabled him to purchase what his modest professorial salary would have made impossible. In addition to the gift of his library, Bruce left a bequest of five thousand dollars, the income of which over the past sixty years has enabled the library to purchase many needed items. Thus Bruce has the claim to be the first of the benefactors of the English Department and one of the earliest benefactors of the

University.   Incidentally, the Bruce gift increased the
total number of books in the library by over ten per cent!
    The final service which Bruce performed for the
Department was the employment of John C. Hodges in 1921.
Hodges had the choice between Tennessee and Duke, and he
chose Tennessee because of the presence of Bruce and his
fine library.   Dr. Hodges always held Bruce in high esteem
and in his office kept a photograph of him and a small desk
that had once belonged to Bruce.   The desk is still owned
by the Department.
    When Assistant Professor Skeffington left in 1905 her
place was taken by Samuel Lee Wolff (1874-1941), who stayed
for two years.   Wolff, a graduate of Harvard and Columbia,
returned to Columbia after leaving Tennessee, and was listed
as an assistant professor in the MLA membership list of
1937.   One of his students, Herman Work, 1909, remembered
Wolff vividly in a speech which he gave to the Forum Club in
Staunton, Virginia, on November 17, 1957.   His students
called him "Brer Wolff."   He "wore a derby hat as well as a
mustache and carried a cane on Sundays: also an air of
slight disdain, not unnoted by his rustic charges."   Work's
description of Freshman English will have a familiar ring to
all who have either taken or taught the course.

> He had some rigid rules . . . each with a
> number, that we had to copy and remember . . .
> when a big pencil mark on a theme indicated
> that No. 7 or 9, or another had been violated.
> Did anyone ever stop to imagine what a task it
> was for the instructor to decipher the erratic
> writing and spot the obvious deficiencies?
> Many a long evening must have been spent in
> such labors.   Once in a while there would be a
> few words of commendation.   As it happened all
> the rules were excellent.   Perhaps many of the
> students were glad later, as I was, that we had
> been held to a sound, sensible pattern that was
> designed centuries before we were born, and not
> merely to annoy us.

    In addition to themes the farmer/engineers were
exposed to Palgrave's Golden Treasury, and for a few it was

a Golden Vision. Work comments on several poems and quotes
lines from Burns, Shakespeare's sonnets, Milton's Lycidas
and the sonnet on his blindness, Thomson's "Rule
Britannia." Work concluded that "Robbie Burns had the
right touch for our Tennessee plowboys who understood what
he was saying because he talked of things they knew about."
Work's career was in forestry, and he was one student for
whom "Brer Wolff" succeeded in overcoming an initial
resistance to composition and poetry. We hope there were
others.

John Thompson Brown, another Virginia graduate,
succeeded Wolff in 1907 and remained until December, 1911,
when he resigned. In addition to Freshman English Brown
taught a one-year survey of English literature for Junior
agricultural and engineering students and a course in
argumentation and debate. Increasing enrollments made
possible the appointment of a third professor in 1909;
Charles Bell Burke, a Cornell Ph.D., whose dissertation,
The Open Road, was the first doctoral dissertation on Walt
Whitman. Burke was placed in charge of sub-freshman English
and the regular freshman course. At the junior-senior level
he introduced new courses in the short story, the essay, and
the novel. A few years later Burke taught a course in
grammar for prospective teachers and a full-year course, the
Age of Tennyson. Since Dr. Burke headed the Department for
almost twenty years following the death of Bruce in 1923, I
shall say more of him in a later chapter.

By 1909 the staff had increased to three professors
assisted by a rapidly shifting group of low-paid
instructors, teaching fellows, and assistants. This
pattern, with greatly increased numbers, has continued to
the present day.

In 1911 George Herbert Clarke (1873-1953) joined the
Department as an associate professor (promoted to professor
the following year) and is, with Kent, Henneman, and Bruce,
one of four professors in the English Department before 1920
to have more than a local reputation. Clarke, a Canadian,
educated at McMaster University, had taught in the U.S.
since 1901: at Mercer and Peabody (1908-11), at the Summer
School of the South on the U.T. campus, and in summer school
at Virginia and Cornell. Clarke was a poet and essayist of
considerable range and ability and had, it could be argued,

the finest purely literary (apart from scholarly) talent of
any one on the Department's roster.   After leaving the
University in 1919, he went to the University of the South
as professor of English and editor of the Sewanee Review.
In 1925 Clarke went to Canada as head of the English
Department of Queen's University and later was editor of the
Queen's Quarterly.   After his death in 1953, at the age of
eighty, tributes poured in attesting to his personal,
professional, editorial, and literary abilities.   In his
later years many honors and honorary degrees came to him.
Thomas R. Gilmore, 1922, recalled Clarke as a professor whom
he particularly remembered.   In Freshman English "he did
something for me that I didn't think would ever happen.
When I got through with that course, I had some appreciation
for English literature I hadn't had before--oh, boy, he was
good.   Now, it's too bad the University had to lose that
man."   I remember that Miss Eleanor Burke, who may have been
a student of Clarke, spoke favorably of him as a member of
the Department who had gone to Sewanee.

Clarke taught a freshman English course for
agricultural and engineering students, which included a
segment on American literature; a history of English
literature (a one-year course), and a year-long course in
Victorian and modern drama, a course later to become one of
the most popular in the Department.

Clarke published his poetry in several magazines.   His
four published volumes were At the Shrine (1914), published
while he was at the University; Wayfarings (1901); The
Hasting Day (1930); Halt and Parley (1934).   After his death
a selection of his poems was published in the Ryerson
Editions of Canadian Poets with an introduction by George
Whalley and W. O. Raymond.   The best way to indicate the
nature and quality of his poetic gift is by quoting two
poems, both on literary topics; one "serious" and the other
slightly satiric.   His poetry is not innovative in style or
subject as is the work of such moderns as Sandburg, Pound or
Eliot.   It is rather more in the style of Thomas Hardy.
Clarke's technical skill was formidable, and he tried most
poetic forms.

"Storm Still"
(Lear)

Wasting the moors, and through the forest glooms,
While thunder booms,
  The skies are streaming;
 With instant glares the darkness shivers,
Each tortured bough thrashes and quivers,--
  The birds are blown by, scudding, screaming.

Stricken lies Love, defeated, ghostly cold,
While on the wold
  An old king stumbles,
Braving the angry batteries of Heaven,
Though planets drown, the giant oaks are riven,
  And the world crumbles.

Storm still, storm over, until the dooms are done
And, one by one,
  The pure stars glow
Upon a wraith-like pair who rise together,
Momently float and fade through moonlit heather,
  Communing close of what no man may know.

(At the Shrine, 1914)

The second poem, addressed to Jane Austen, reminds us that Miss Austen was not in 1914 the popular novelist she has become during the twentieth century.

TO MISS JANE AUSTEN

Madam, I must express respectful wonder
  At your delightful novels, penned despite
Your unawareness of the proper thunder
Employed by those professionals who write
  For present generations.

You've minor merits; we have--Miss Corelli--
  She's in "Who's Who" and so is Mistress Ward;

Your heroines are <u>bourgeoise</u> Liz or Nellie--
   Such homely English hearts you seem to hoard,
   Untoned by foreign nations.

Your canvas, too, is very small and shrinking--
   You've said as much yourself--and yet you
      smile,
Content with gentle raillery, not thinking
   Of what you <u>ought</u> to do--belabour guile
     With stageable gyrations.

Indeed, dear Madam Jane, the eagle wheeling,
   The vulture tearing, e'en the owl sedate,
Or brooding hen,--such modern modes of feeling
   Are foreign to you, I regret to state
     (With mental reservations).

So mild and unobtrusive seems your pleasure
   It minds us rather of the humming-bird,
Sipping and skimming to a patterned measure,
   Within an ordered park of way and word,
     'Mid Spring's felicitations.

It's true, of course, that you amused Sir Walter,
   Lewes, Macaulay, and a number more,
But fashions change, Miss Austen, <u>have</u> to alter,--
   Your glowworm humour now is ancient lore,
     Barren of imitations.

In short, although we like you still extremely,
   It's not the thing to read you nowadays;
If only you had been a bit unseemly
   In style, or bold of plot, why then our praise
     Might still perform oblations.

So good-bye, Madam; we must leave behind us
   Your wit and wisdom, for no more they'll do:
We must progress, the publishers remind us--
   This chat was pleasant, but it means--adieu!--
     <u>Our</u> people are creations.

                  (<u>At the Shrine, 1914</u>)

It would be pleasant to end the chapter of the Ayres presidency and the departure of Professor Clarke on a happy note, but unfortunately I cannot. The story of his dismissal is as follows. On January 28, 1919 President Ayres died suddenly, and Dean Hoskins served as acting president from February to July when the trustees elected Morgan to the presidency. Hoskins was promoted from Dean of Liberal Arts to the new post of Dean of the University and assistant to the president, but retained his title of Dean of Liberal Arts. In the winter of 1919 the state legislature passed a law that no person not a citizen of the U.S. could be employed by the state of Tennessee, but that present employees would have until 1925 to comply with the law. Clarke was not the only one at U.T. affected. Like Clarke, Harcourt Morgan was also a Canadian, but he promptly applied for citizenship. Clarke, hesitating to take this important step, consulted Nashville and Knoxville attorneys who assured him that the statute gave him time before he must take appropriate action. When Clarke returned to the campus in September, however, Dean Hoskins and President Morgan told him that he had no position although his name had been published in the catalog for the coming year and courses assigned to him. Clarke appealed this decision in a letter which is spread upon the minutes of the Board of Trustees for the meeting of November 27, 1919. Clarke stressed that he had not been notified prior to the opening of the academic year and that academic positions were difficult to find so late in the year. But the trustees, acting upon the advice of the attorney general, supported the new administration by a narrow majority: 7, yes; 4, no; 1, abstention. The minutes give no hint of what was said at the meeting, but the close vote shows that several trustees were dubious about the wisdom of the action. The new president, always sensitive about questions of his citizenship, would not have pushed the issue since he was still a Canadian citizen, U.S. citizenship not being granted him until the following year. Clarke received $555.55 "in full settlement and satisfaction of any claim" against the University. Clarke's receipt of $555.55 represented his salary for two and two-thirds months. Clarke's salary of $2,500.00 came to $208.33 per month so that the sum of $555.55 represents the months of September

and October plus two-thirds of November, give or take a few
pennies. This careful computation of pay down to fractions
of a month continued for many years--perhaps it still does.
Today, Clarke would have had a choice of legal remedies, but
fortunately for him, he immediately found a position at the
University of the South. In this instance, the University,
not Clarke, was the loser. He went on to enjoy a career far
more distinguished and satisfying than he could have had at
U.T. The Hoskins-Morgan administration clearly had no wish
to keep the services of a talented professor with eight
years of service or to show appreciation for his
achievement. As the first administrative action of the new
"team" it did not augur well for faculty welfare.

CHAPTER IV

THE TWENTIES: GROWTH AND CHANGE

The first post-war year (1919-20) saw a marked increase in enrollment on the Knoxville campus from 572 to 960. Without the services of Professor Clarke, Bruce and Burke must have had difficulty in coping with a seventy per cent increase in enrollment.   Miss Josephine Reddish, who had taught English since 1907 as teaching fellow and instructor, was now promoted for one year to assistant professor.   (The following year she moved on to the math department.)   The rest of the staff consisted of instructors and assistants. In 1920, however, new appointments strengthened the department.   Allan H. Gilbert, a Harvard Ph.D., came as professor taking Clarke's place, and Miss Mamie C. Johnston was appointed an assistant professor.   Marguerite B. Hamer served for one year as an assistant professor of English and history and then moved to the history department on a full-time basis.   Since Miss Johnston and Dr. Hamer remained at the University until their retirements, many readers of this history will recall them.

1920-21 brought further changes.   Gilbert resigned and went to Duke University.   In his place Bruce employed John C. Hodges, another Harvard Ph.D., and then associate professor of English at Ohio Wesleyan.   But Miss Johnston, who had enjoyed the rank of assistant professor during the previous year, was now listed as an instructor--a rank which she held throughout her long career.   Although Miss Johnston had studied at the University of Chicago, she never received a Ph.D.   It is evident that in the English Department that degree was now a prerequisite for any rank above that of instructor.   Another first appointment as instructor should be mentioned--that of Miss Louise Wiley, who taught for several years in the 1920s and then returned in the 1940s to help the Department cope with the great increase in enrollment after World War II.   She was then Mrs. McCleary, and is still remembered as a generous friend of the University and a gracious hostess in her home on Scenic Drive.

Course changes and assignments inevitably followed staff changes.   The most notable was the assignment of Hodges as supervisor of the rapidly increasing work in

Freshman English, which had been Burke's assignment since 1909. This appointment was to have great impact upon every one in the Department and the University, whether as student or professor, as it was from his teaching and direction of the Freshman English program that the Harbrace College Handbook emerged. Hodges established the freshman work as a serious aspect of the departmental program, and this emphasis upon its importance assisted the Department greatly in its relations with other departments and colleges.

The increasing number of students each year made it possible to introduce new subjects and courses and to increase the number of instructors. In 1923-24 a course in journalism was taught by Instructor James W. Painter. This course remained in the Department until it was transferred to the College of Business Administration and later to its own school and college. The same year also saw the introduction of a course in argumentation, the beginning of the program in public speaking. The instructors of these two courses changed almost annually.

The death of Bruce in the winter of 1923 left one of the three professorships of English vacant. Hodges recommended his old Harvard friend, Alwin Thaler, then an assistant professor at the University of California at Berkeley, to fill the vacancy. In 1927 another senior appointment was made: Roscoe E. Parker, a medievalist, and a California Ph.D. These three--Hodges, Thaler, and Parker--were the mainstay of the Department for two or three decades, and to them the present Department owes a great debt for creating the Department that we know and the scholarly atmosphere that has prevailed. The professorial staff taught the advanced work, but most of the freshman and sophomore teaching was performed by a constantly changing group of instructors and by four teaching fellows who taught two sections of Freshman English each quarter while studying for an M.A.

The coming of Parker in 1927 enabled the Department to offer courses in medieval literature that had been dropped after Bruce's death. Parker also offered quarter courses in expository writing, the history of the English language, and the teaching of English, in addition to a year-long course in medieval English literature. In 1929 John B. Emperor joined the Department as an assistant professor and quickly won a secure place for himself with students and colleagues. He assumed responsibility for the program in public speaking and comparative literature, his one-quarter course in Greek and Roman literature in translation becoming one of the most popular advanced courses, one which, after Emperor's death, I continued.

Although many instructors stayed for only a year or two, Broadus Farrar, who came in 1925, remained for several years until he went to serve as the head of the Department at the University of Tennessee at Martin, then a Junior College. He returned later to Knoxville where he taught for many years in the Evening School and the Extension Division, and is fondly remembered by many former students and University associates.

With the vacant professorship created by the death of Bruce going to Thaler, the senior professor, Dr. Burke, received the headship of the small but rapidly growing department. When Burke arrived on the campus fourteen years earlier in 1909, he was placed in charge of freshman English and taught most of the freshmen in the University. No student, however, had a good word either for the course or the professor. Joseph Wood Krutch, whose luke-warm description of Bruce has been quoted, was devastating about Burke, who required that students memorize long excerpts from Genung's Rhetoric. He describes Burke as "a rather fierce little man with a mustache waxed in military fashion and by temperament both frantically respectable and a martinet." Every Friday each student recited some verses he had memorized. Krutch thought to shock Burke by quoting from Omar and Walt Whitman, but since Burke's dissertation had been on Whitman, I doubt that Burke was shocked. Shocked or not, Burke awarded Krutch, a hard-working student, an A in the course. Burke was a notoriously hard grader, almost never gave an A, and had once remarked that he would not have given Edgar Allan Poe more than a B or B+! President Hoskins' sketch of Burke, which comes at the end of his complimentary sketches of Kent and Bruce, is both lengthy and condemnatory:

Dr. Burke when he first came to the institution had charge of Freshman English and was one of the most rigid teachers in the institution. In fact he was so rigid that students dreaded to take his English. All Freshmen are required to take English and more students failed under him than under any professor in years .... For a number of years about a third of the class would pass Freshman English. He taught Genung's Rhetoric and students dreaded this subject more than any other. I also told him that when a teacher found that year after year less than 50% of his class passed his subject, there must be something wrong with the teacher. His method of teaching was memoriter method. For example, on examination he would ask students to begin at the tenth line from the last line of some poem and quote it from there on. This I think was a serious mistake and told him so. I tried to get President Ayres to allow students to choose their teachers in Freshman English. Professor George H. Clarke taught one section of Freshman English but President Ayres would not make the change and the majority of the students were required to take Burke's course. When Dr. Ayres died in 1919 and President Morgan became his successor, I requested President Morgan to get another teacher of Freshman English and change the method of instruction. To move Dr. Burke to subjects beyond the Freshman class because I thought a student should have been in the University at least a year before he studied under Dr. Burke.

This change took place when Hodges came to the University, and Hoskins approved it as a "very important change that has proved satisfactory." Although Dr. Burke no longer taught freshmen, he continued his severe methods with upperclassmen until his enrollments dropped to eight, whereupon Dean Hoskins issued an ultimatum and told Dean Porter (of Liberal Arts) to confer with Dr. Burke "and tell him that if the number of students continued to drop we would have to get another professor. Dr. Burke changed then and thereafter became more popular and an effective teacher of English."

Burke remained as head from 1923 to 1942, but for the last seven years of his tenure Hodges served as the de facto head under the title of associate head. If the appointment of Burke in 1909 was unfortunate for the Department and the University (as the preceding statement by Hoskins strongly suggests), his appointment as head was equally unfortunate. If the University had had any retirement system, Burke could have retired in 1933 at sixty-five after only ten years in the position, but economic necessity forced him to continue for another decade. In 1942 the University agreed to pension a group of professors who were still at their posts well into their seventies and even eighties. The pension, paid from the general fund, was forty per cent of the last salary, which in Dr. Burke's case was forty per cent of $4,200.00. Prior to that time a retiree or one dismissed from his post lived on his savings. The good old days were not always good!

Coming as he did between Bruce and Hodges, Burke's deficiencies were all the more striking. The reputation of his classroom teaching and his lack of scholarly achievement did not command the respect that his position required. Burke, however, was not without positive qualities. Outside the classroom and with his colleagues Dr. Burke presented a genial side. He was unfailingly polite, his manners were courtly, and he enjoyed good conversation with friends and associates. His ideal was that of the traditional Southern gentleman, whose word was as good as his bond. His father had been a captain in the Army of the Confederacy, and as a consequence he was always conscious of his Southern heritage. Politically, he was a staunch Democrat and a supporter of the New Deal and the TVA. I never saw any sign of personal jealousy towards his colleagues. He genuinely rejoiced in the achievements of others. I remember he was especially pleased with the publication of Hodges' Congreve for the recognition its publication would bring the author and the Department, and similarly with the publications of Thaler, Parker, even articles by one of the instructors (I speak here for myself as well as others). In contrast, many professors in other departments pooh-poohed scholarly publication as a waste of time that should be spent teaching students. Burke also sought to upgrade the quality of the faculty by taking advantage of the buyers' market during the depression by employing Ph.D.s. Before 1933 there were no Ph.D. instructors. Two things can thus be said in Burke's favor: he respected and encouraged scholarship in the

Department and sought well-qualified Ph.D.s from the leading graduate schools to fill vacant positions rather than doing the easy thing by giving the jobs to the University's recently minted M.A.s.

My own personal relations with Dr. Burke were always amiable, and he was on several occasions quite confidential and told me incidents of the early years of the Department and University. I do not think he had any particular friends, and he always impressed me as an essentially cold person. The result was that, put quite simply, he was not liked. He lived with his semi-invalid daughter Eleanor in a large gloomy house at 1635 Laurel Avenue, the site of the present Barclay House apartments. On his retirement in 1942, he sold his home and moved to Florida, where the climate proved beneficial to his arthritis. For a few years after he left Knoxville he wrote poetry, which he sent back to the office for the secretary, Mrs. Mildred George, to type. He died in 1953 at the age of eighty-five, and his daughter survived him by only a few years. Before his retirement he funded two awards: the Captain Robert A. Burke Award for excellence in prose fiction in honor of his father and the Eleanora R. Burke Award for excellence in expository writing in honor of his wife, who had died in 1936.

Thus far in this fourth chapter I have confined my remarks to changes in staff, new courses in the English curriculum, and a sketch of Dr. Burke, but it is now appropriate to look at the turbulent events that swirled about the Department both within the University and in the state during this decade. The two events to which I refer are, first, the firing of seven professors (none in English) in 1923 and the subsequent investigation of the University by the American Association of University Professors with all its attendant national publicity, and, second, the Scopes trial in 1925 which brought more unfavorable national publicity, not only to the state but to the University. Some of this censure of the University came from its own alumnus and English major, Joseph Wood Krutch. The chapter is to close with a sketch of the president, Harcourt A. Morgan (1919-1933), and which is necessary to understand why, despite increased appropriations for the University and the boom-like prosperity of the nation, state, and Knoxville, the English Department and other academic departments struggled under conditions no better, perhaps worse, than during the preceding decade.

The end of World War I and the unexpected death of President Ayres in 1919 brought an old era to an end. The boom years of the 1920s brought increased enrollments and large appropriations from the legislature, but all was not quiet in the University. Harcourt A. Morgan, Dean of the College of Agriculture, won the coveted post of president from his rival, James D. Hoskins, Dean of the College of Liberal Arts and disciplinarian of the students. In the ensuing allocation of administrative responsibilities, Hoskins filled the newly created post of Dean of the University and tended to the internal affairs of the institution, while Morgan, a superb politician, spent much time away from the campus wooing the rural legislators whom he knew from his days as Dean of Agriculture and in active promotion of programs in Agricultural Extension and Experiment Stations throughout the state. Where Ayres had avoided quarrels and confrontation, Hoskins, and perhaps Morgan, seemed to invite trouble. His first action as dean and acting president had been the abrupt dismissal of the able English professor, George Herbert Clarke, who had given good service for eight years. In 1923 a major brouhaha emerged with the firing of the seven professors: A. A. Schaeffer, head of zoology, Maurice Mulvania, head of bacteriology and adviser to pre-medical students; R. S. Radford, professor of Latin; J. W. Sprowls, assistant professor of secondary eduction; Robert S. Ellis, professor of psychology and philosophy; Mrs. Ada Withers, assistant professor of art; and the colorful and dynamic John R. Neal, the popular professor of law. A reading of Montgomery and Greene reveals as much of this procedure as can be ascertained several decades later, but the local, state, and national publicity, and the consequent report and investigation by the American Association of University Professors did nothing to enhance the reputation of the University as an enlightened center of academic life. The New York Times followed the incident closely, and devoted a special story to it in a Sunday supplement.

It is scarcely worthwhile to assess blame, the AAUP

report suggesting that there may have been some justification for the dismissals, but that the way in which it was done was insensitive and inhumane. Schaeffer, like Clarke, returned at the end of a summer research trip to find that he had been fired. The dismissed professors as a group were not neophytes but had several years of service at the University to their credit. Four of the seven are to be found in editions of Who Was Who, held Ph.D.s from prestigious universities (Schaeffer and Radford from Johns Hopkins, Mulvania from Wisconsin, and Neal from Columbia), and several later found positions at good institutions. Schaeffer went to the University of Kansas, Radford to Kenyon College, and Mulvania to Florida Southern College, where he held a responsible post in the successful eradication of the Mediterranean fruit fly in 1929 (curiously, Morgan was also involved in this program!). Neal, a wealthy man, founded his own law school, which proved to be a competitive threat to the University's law school. The four just mentioned were research and publication-minded faculty (as was Clarke). The conclusion must be that the wholesale firing can be attributed to the inability of Hoskins and Morgan to withstand the petty and annoying fault-finding and criticism that every administrator usually learns to live with. Sad to say, able persons would have been aware of the educational shortcomings of Hoskins and Morgan, neither one of whom had a Ph.D. or graduate study at a leading university as had their predecessors Dabney and Ayres.

After the local newspapers and the students, through their underground newspaper the Independent Truth, had forgotten the episode as the fired professors left the campus and found employment elsewhere, a new issue came to plague Morgan and engage the University in controversy: the introduction and passage in 1925 of the anti-evolution law. Since President McVey of the University of Kentucky had led a successful fight to defeat a similar bill introduced into the Kentucky legislature three years before, many persons within the state looked to President Morgan to lead a similar fight in Tennessee. But after much soul-searching Morgan decided against upsetting "the delicate financial harmony existing between the University and the legislature." (Montgomery, p. 42) Morgan did not wish to jeopardize the gains in public support for the University from the legislature by jumping into this controversy. The faculty, who had learned their lessons well in 1923, chose silence as the better part of valor, and since such outspoken professors as Schaeffer and Radford were no longer on campus there was no one left to speak up.

Evidence suggests that Morgan thought the bill would be ignored, and professors at the University would--and did--go on teaching evolution as they had been doing (and as Morgan himself had done during his teaching days). But no one could have foreseen the Scopes Trial, which broke out immediately and brought the world press to the small town of Dayton, and through newspaper, book, play, and film has made the issue and the state of Tennessee a by-word for backwardness throughout the world.

The firings of 1923 arose in interesting form in connection with the Scopes Trial. One of the chief lawyers for the defense was none other than the dismissed Professor John R. Neal, who assumed the defense of Scopes and also secured the assistance of the famed lawyer Clarence Darrow. Another ghost from the past also came on the scene at the trial--the young reporter, Joseph Wood Krutch, a graduate of the University, who had been threatened with expulsion by Dean Hoskins for the writing of a controversial article in the student magazine. As a reporter for the Nation, and now established as a member of the New York literary establishment, he had his chance to expose the University and its leadership in his articles, and much later in his autobiography, More Lives than One.

Because there are so few surviving reminiscences of the University from these years, Krutch's writings are frequently quoted to give the reader an idea of the temper of the times. Even after a liberal discounting of the journalistic hyperbole in which Krutch bathed his articles--including his title "Tennessee: Where Cowards Rule"--there resides a core of truth in Krutch's words: "The legislator is afraid of some fundamentalist in the mountains; the president is afraid of the legislature; the faculty is afraid of the president; and the newspaper editor is afraid of someone who is afraid of someone who is afraid of someone else." The evolution bill had been introduced by a primitive Baptist from a rural county; Morgan was afraid to

oppose the bill because of his fear that the legislature
would in turn reject his bid for increased appropriations
for the University; and the faculty, after their experience
with the wholesale firings of 1923, had every reason to be
afraid of the president and the dean. In fact, for many
years newcomers to the campus observed that the faculty
were careful not to offend, and it was not uncommon as late
as the 1950s for someone to remark on how many people seemed
afraid of someone else.

To understand the milieu in which the English
Department lived we must consider the relations of the
Department with the presidents. We have seen that
Presidents Dabney and Ayres had sought to make strong
appointments in the English Department and recognized the
importance of live, vigorous programs in all the academic
departments of the University. This happy time came to an
abrupt end with the unexpected death of President Ayres in
1919 and the appointment of the Dean of Agriculture,
Harcourt A. Morgan (1867-1950) to the presidency. A skilful
politician, Morgan had come to the University in 1905 as
director of the Agricultural Experiment Station, then became
Dean of the College of Agriculture in 1913, and president in
1919. Thomas K. McCraw in his article on Morgan in the
Dictionary of American Biography reveals both Morgan's
strengths and weaknesses. During his fourteen years the
enrollment increased from fewer than eight hundred to more
than five thousand (including the medical units at Memphis).
"He himself excelled as a manager of the university's
external relations, rather than as a leader of faculty or
students . . . . and established a relationship with
successive governors that brought generous state
appropriations." Morgan was a man with a mission, a mission
which he worked out in a philosophy which he called the
common mooring. "In his view, mankind had begun to
interfere dangerously with the earth's ecosystems . . . the
root sin in this ominous process was man's failure to
perceive the essential and delicate unity of nature--the
interdependence ('common mooring') of all life." His
appointment in 1933--and his resignation as president of the
University--as a director of TVA enabled him to put his
dream into practice. His dream was and still is a noble
one, but in pursuing this cause, he, like so many men and

women dedicated to noble causes, subordinated all else. In Morgan's case it was to neglect or ignore the many other roles and "causes" to which the University and its faculty were devoted. His position became only a means of furthering his own vision. He thus left the running of the University to Dean Hoskins, knew few of the faculty and students, and spent most of his time talking to farm groups and successfully lobbying legislators and governors. There is no evidence (in the DAB article) that Morgan ever sought to advance other programs in the University. A measure of the regard in which Morgan was held was the comment that the best thing TVA did for the University was to make Morgan a director! The general impression in the mid-thirties after his departure from the presidency was that Morgan had taken no interest in the academic programs or in the welfare of the faculty.

The only anecdote concerning Morgan and the English Department and the faculty I know and which corroborates the statements of the preceding paragraph was a story that Dr. Burke told me a year or two before his retirement. Soon after Morgan assumed the presidency a group of senior professors, seven or eight, including Burke and Bruce, called on Morgan and expressed their concern and wish that salaries be increased (all full professors received the same salary of $3,250 per year) and that other measures be taken to improve the cultural and educational ambience of the University. Morgan's reply to the senior professors was that he had no interest in doing anything, and that if they were unhappy with the way things were at the University they should seek employment elsewhere. In other words, the faculty as employees of the administration were not to be involved with decision-making, and served only at the pleasure of the president and deans. Decisions were made at the top. Such attitudes were by no means uncommon, and were the norm in those days at most colleges and universities.

A superb politician and a dynamo of energy, Morgan did gain support from governmental agencies, but the evidence appears that the major portion of the money went to strengthen the agricultural programs throughout the state and on the campus. It certainly did not trickle down to the English Department or the Library. One result of this administrative effort to further the agricultural programs was that for years critics of the University (especially those in Nashville) condescendingly referred to the University as a "cow college"--an epithet the institution has had difficulty in living down, despite its remarkable advances in all fields during the last thirty-five or forty years. The Morgan legacy is not one the English Department can look back upon with pride or satisfaction. Morgan was a remarkable man, with the greatly admired virtue of being able to get things done, but the things he wanted done were not so much the development of the academic programs within the University, the College of Liberal Arts, and the English Department, but rather of improving the soils and ecology of the South and the state of Tennessee.

Notes

A quick survey of the enrollment numbers and the numbers of senior faculty reveals the measure of neglect the Department suffered. In 1913 the Department had three full professors (Bruce, Burke, and Clarke) when the enrollment was less than a thousand. In 1922 the enrollment on the Knoxville campus was 1,096. There were then still three professors and three instructors. By 1926-27 the enrollment had grown to 1,774 as the number of professors remained at three, but the number of instructors had increased to thirteen. By 1929 the students on the Knoxville campus had increased to 2,471, and the professorial staff had increased to five with the addition of one associate professor and one assistant professor. It is clear that the English Department was not sharing in the rapid growth of the University nor of the generous appropriations granted by the legislature. The beneficiary of the prosperity of the 1920s was clearly the agricultural units, particularly the growing state-wide programs of agricultural extension and the growth of the agricultural experiment stations. For most of the nineteen-twenties Burke, Thaler, and Hodges taught the advanced courses, the majors and minors in English, and supervised the programs for the large numbers of students in the freshman and sophomore courses. The teaching was done by a largely peripatetic group of low-paid instructors, not all of whom had M.A.s. This was no way to build a corps of professionals, but the choice was not that of the professors of English but of the deans and the president.

Bruce, Burke, Hodges, Knickerbocker

Professors—1975
Bottom Row: Curry, Drake, Davis, Fisher, Adams, Miller,
Spivey, Wright
Top row: Hansen, Sanders, Stewart, Wheeler, Kelly

44

Associate Professors—1975
Bottom Row: Ensor, Walker, Dumas, Bratton, Leggett
Top Row: Gill, Penner, Carroll

Assistant Professors and tenured Instructors—1975
Bottom Row: Cox, Armistead, D. Goslee, Goode, Gaines, Lofaro
Top row: Koger, Badgett, Martin, Hammontree, N. Goslee,
Burghardt

Professors—1988
Bottom Row: Penner, Drake, Schneider, Wheeler, N. Goslee, Trahern, Cox, Ensor, Kelly, Armistead, Scura, Leggett, Sanders
Top Row: Shurr, Miller, Bratton, Heffernan, Lofaro, Carroll

Associate Professors—1988
Bottom Row: Gill, Dumas, D. Goslee, Hutchinson, Stillman
Top Row: Burghardt, Maland, Leki, Keene

Assistant Professors—1988
Bottom Row: Campbell, Zomchick, Papke, Bensel-Meyers,
Hammontree, Riley, Smith
Top Row: Wallace, Dunn, Samson

Instructors—1988
Bottom Row: Berry, Rees, Ball, Overbey, Lighter, von Brentano,
Hardwig, Peavler, Powell, Datz, Aiken, Bensen, Rohloff,
Waldvogel, Demastes, Williamson, Clark, Combe
Top Row: Emery, McKinstry, Adler, Lee, Hanse, Ringer,
Grieve-Carlson, Tschantz, Sherwood, Lewis, Fogelman, Wheatley,
Tanenbaum

47

Professorial Staff—1988
Bottom Row: Gill, Drake, Penner, Armistead, Riley, Leggett,
N. Goslee, Smith, Hammontree, Dumas, Stillman, Zomchick,
Bensel-Meyers, Papke, Bratton, Scura, Campbell, Trahern,
Hutchinson, Leki, Cox, Maland, Sanders, Kelly
Top Row: Miller, Keene, Wallace, Samson, Wheeler, Schneider,
Ensor, Dunn, D. Goslee, Carroll, Lofaro

Secretaries—1988
Giles, Brock, Meredith, Wheeler, Owings, Lewis

CHAPTER V

DEPRESSION AND WAR: 1930-1945

The stock market crash of October 1929 brought the prosperous decade of the twenties to an abrupt end. Its consequences were quickly felt by all segments of business, government, and education as banks failed, businesses and individuals declared bankruptcy, and tax collections plunged. The nearly bankrupt state of Tennessee slashed all budgets including the appropriation for the University. But the University and the English Department did survive, and enrollments held up fairly well.

During the twenties enrollments rose steadily and reached a peak of 2,642 on the Knoxville campus in 1930-31, dropped in 1932-22 to 2,259, and reached a low of 2,031 for the regular session of 1933-34. The percentage of decline in attendance at summer school was more precipitous: from the summer of 1932 to the summer of 1933 the number dropped from 1,499 to 1,031. Because all students were required to enroll in Freshman English there was always work for a corps of instructors, albeit a reduced number. The nine instructors for 1932-33 were reduced to four by 1933-34. But the increase of three hundred students for the year 1934-35 made possible the employment of three new instructors and raised the number to seven. The fall of 1934 witnessed the implementation of Dr. Burke's new policy of filling vacancies with Ph.D. instructors, and since academic jobs during the early 1930s were difficult to find, he had no difficulty in filling the posts. The first three Ph.D. instructors were: Ralph Collins (Yale), who left the following year for Indiana University, where he later became Dean of the Faculty; Clarence C. Green (Harvard), who went to Lehigh University after two years, and John S. Davenport (North Carolina), who stayed for several years as one of the Department's most popular and able instructors before he went to Knox College in Illinois. After 1933-34 the enrollments gained steadily, and Dr. Burke was able to fill the vacant or additional instructorships either with Ph.D.s or those soon to be.

During the early 1930s several important changes in the University and college administration took place. The Dean of Liberal Arts, Dr. James Porter, died on August 27, 1931, and Dr. Philip Hamer, head of the history department, became acting dean. Following Hamer's resignation in 1934 and his acceptance of a post at the National Archives, Dr. Lexemuel R. Hesler, Professor of Botany and head of that Department, assumed the deanship, which he held for twenty-four years until his retirement in 1958 at the age of seventy. In 1933, as already noted, President Morgan became a director of TVA to be succeeded in the presidency by Dean Hoskins, who continued as president until 1946 when he resigned at the age of seventy-six. The faculty had hoped that Hoskins would be sympathetic to their interests and to the academic programs, but these hopes were disappointed as the University only marked time for the dozen years of his presidency. A sketch of President Hoskins is included at the end of this chapter because an understanding of his administration--and of Morgan's under whom he served as dean--is necessary to understand the failure of the institution to seize its opportunities and build upon the strengths of the strong departments.

The Department during these years, however, fostered several growing programs that later became independent departments inside and outside the College of Liberal Arts. Instructors in the English Department had taught the course in journalism since the 1920s. Journalism is today a flourishing department of the College of Communications. In 1933-34 Stanley Johnson, the Director of Public Relations, a liaison officer between the University and the legislature (a "lobbyist"), and a speech writer for officials of the administration, took over the course and was given the title of Assistant Professor of English, following the suicide of Instructor Earl Devon on October 28, 1932. Although Johnson taught the course for several years and is listed as a member of the English Department, I never met him, and as far as I know he never attended a staff meeting. Johnson, a Vanderbilt alumnus, was the author of The Professor, a *roman à clef* of the Vanderbilt faculty, and a fringe member of the Fugitive Group, a membership which has guaranteed him a certain immortality.

During the early thirties the program in speech grew in importance under the leadership of John Emperor, who was assisted by various instructors such as Argus Tresidder, Broadus Farrar, C. H. McReynolds, and especially by Paul

Soper, who came to the Department in 1936 and later became the head of the Department of Speech and Theatre when the program achieved the status of an independent department in 1968. The enrollments in the speech courses increased rapidly, especially after some colleges permitted one quarter of public speaking to be substituted for one quarter of the three-quarter sophomore English requirement. We have noted that in the nineteenth and early twentieth centuries debating, under the sponsorship of the student literary societies, flourished with the final debating competition at the end of the year attracting large audiences like the one in 1880 in which William G. McAdoo, Jr., prominently figures. After the passing of the literary societies the Debate Club for many years sponsored several debates, the Department introduced courses in debate and argumentation for college credit, and a member of the Department assisted as a debate coach. The forensics program suffered from a chronic lack of funds. An item from the annual report of 1937-38 illustrates the lengths to which those in charge of forensics had to stoop by the statement that the annual expenses of $90.00 came from gifts from the Student Dance Fund and the Scarabbean Society. By 1940-41 the program in speech had developed so that the Department offered a major in English with emphasis in speech, and in the next year, 1940-41, a minor in speech.

Groups of students and faculty had from time to time formed dramatic clubs and produced plays--the first as early as 1840. The English Department, however, did not become involved in the direction and production of plays until about 1930 when John Emperor and instructor Argus Tresidder coached as an extracurricular effort a group of students who presented several plays. It was not until 1939-40 that the English Department formally assisted the U.T. Playhouse, as the student dramatic group was called, in producing plays when Paul Soper was assigned the responsibility for direction and production. In 1940-41 a one-year course in theatre was introduced into the English curriculum in which acting, stagecraft, and play interpretation and directing were offered. Most of the enrollees in this course had participated in the acting and production of plays on campus, and from this year on the program in theatre grew despite the lack of any adequate facility on campus for the presentation of plays. Most of the productions during the late thirties and forties were given at the auditorium of Tyson Junior High School on Kingston Pike. Not until the erection of the Carousel Theatre, a theatre in the round, in 1951 did the group have its own on-campus facility, and not until 1970 with the erection of the Clarence Brown Theatre did the University have a theatre with a proscenium stage and the necessary facilities for a viable and thriving program. I should emphasize that the production of these first plays depended completely upon the receipts from ticket sales, since no University funds were made available. The Department, with the encouragement of its head, Dr. Hodges, together with the directorship of Paul Soper, assisted in the 1940s and 1950s by Fred Fields and Russell Green, laid the foundations for the present flourishing program in theatre and the creation of the separate Department of Speech and Theatre. These persons, as well as students, faculty, and hundreds of volunteers, town as well as gown, who served as actors, stage hands, scenery painters, and ticket sellers, deserve great credit for initiating this program and sustaining it even against adverse criticism from within and without the University by persons whose lingering distrust of theatre and actors led them to judge all plays and players to be just slightly immoral.

Not all the encouragement of drama was in the realm of play production. In the spring of 1935 the Department sponsored a playwriting contest for the best one-act play. The winning play was written by Dorothy Romines, as James Chandler and John Baugh (later a professor of law and secretary of the Board of Trustees) tied for second place. The three plays were staged on May 22 in the Alumni Memorial Auditorium. Other play-writing contests were held from time to time with the prize-winning plays given a production by the U. T. Playhouse.

The Department established an English Writing Laboratory during the winter and spring quarters of 1937 in answer to requests from students and faculty who sought help for their students with problems in composition. The laboratory in its first years had three two-hour sessions each week and an experienced instructor was in charge. The students received individual instruction for whatever problems they were having. Although some came voluntarily, others were sent by an instructor in the English Department who gave the student an incomplete grade which would be removed after a series of remedial visits and the submission of several satisfactory themes. Students who came voluntarily could enter at any time during the quarter and leave whenever they felt that they had achieved their objectives. Some who came during the first quarter were: a student who was writing an historical drama in verse, an agricultural student who wanted assistance for a paper he was entering in a nation-wide contest for agricultural students, and others came because an instructor had suggested that the laboratory could help them in improving their skills in composition. An occasional graduate student came for assistance in writing an M.A. thesis in a technical field. The Writing Laboratory was informally structured, and because of this informality was able to respond to the needs of the individual. The laboratory proved to be a popular, worthwhile service of the Department, has been continued to the present day, and expanded to several sections. Unfortunately, the laboratory has always been an easy target for retrenchment when financial crises hit the University, and the Department has often been forced to reduce drastically the services which the laboratory offers the collegiate community.

Except for changes in enrollment and personnel in the Department and the growth of the programs in public speaking and theatre, there is really little to record for the years covered by this chapter. The changes were all made within the limitations of a small budget and did not call for the employment of senior staff or appropriations for special equipment. The Department was staffed by able persons, still in their prime, and the work of instruction was faithfully, conscientiously, and competently performed under conditions that can only be described as discouraging. The drastic cuts in state support and the decline in enrollments at the beginning of the depression made cuts in salary inevitable. Thaler reports that there were three cuts totalling twenty per cent, and these were not restored until about 1939. The University, however, paid its salaries and on time as the treasurer, J. J. Walker, proudly told historians Montgomery and Greene. Since many colleges were unable to meet their payrolls either completely or in timely fashion (the Knoxville city teachers were receiving their salaries in scrip), the faculty did not grumble as might be expected. All were poor together!

During those lean years no saving could be ignored. The University economized in all possible ways. The Library had no money for new books for several years, but Miss Mary Baker, the Librarian, wisely spent the limited income from a few small endowments to continue serials. Maintenance of buildings virtually stopped. Windows may have been washed once a year, and I can remember in the late 1930s that some of the classrooms in Ayres Hall still had broken windowpanes into which cardboard had been placed to keep out the winter cold. When better days came, the University had a great deal of catching up to do in every sphere.

This catching up, however, had to await the passing of another national crisis: World War II. A partial recovery in the University's fortunes took place during the years 1937 through 1941 which partly repaired the ravages of the depression. Enrollments in the University declined steadily as the war dragged on, but enrollments in English held up much better than in other departments because all students were required to take Freshman English. During the fall of 1938 enrollment in all freshman courses was 757, and in the fall of 1944 it had only dropped to 665. The enrollment, however, in the sophomore courses dropped more drastically from 529 in the fall of 1938 to 307 in the fall of 1944, a decline of almost fifty per cent.

During 1942-43 Dr. Hodges became actively engaged in the Statewide English Program to be sponsored by the Tennessee Council of Teachers of English, designed to improve the quality of English teaching throughout the schools of Tennessee. By collecting the scores of freshmen entering the colleges in the state of Tennessee it was possible to identify the high schools with superior programs in English as well as the superior teachers of high-school English. Dr. Hodges himself visited many schools and began a program that was to be expanded after the war when the Department employed Charles F. Webb as an instructor of English (he later became an Associate Professor) to teach for the Department during the fall term when enrollments were highest, and during the winter and spring to visit

schools throughout the state. This successful program
continued until Professor Webb's retirement in 1970. The
role of the University in trying to assist the schools of
the state through a program of visitation from professors in
the University was an old one. In the 1890s Professors
Kent, Henneman, and especially Karns visited schools
throughout the state. Hodges was thus reviving an ancient
custom.

The sharp decline in student enrollments at the
University as the war continued caused the administration
great concern, but the arrival of 1,200 Air Force trainees
in March, 1943, helped alleviate the stringent situation.

> Under the air cadet operation, the University would
> train 1,200 cadets every five months. The Air Force
> men, who would arrive in Knoxville after five weeks of
> basic training, would then receive five months of
> instruction in English, mathematics, current history,
> geography, physics, physical education, medical aid,
> and military drill. (Montgomery, Threshold of a New
> Day, p.374)

The University designed the curriculum to conform to
government specifications, but the courses did not carry
collegiate credit. The program proved a boon to faculty in
departments which had suffered severe drops in enrollment as
the University mobilized the skills and talents of all the
faculty throughout the University. The detachment of air-
corps cadets remained until June 30, 1944.

The annual report for 1943-44 gives the details of
this program as it affected the English Department. Since
most of the members of the Department were already fully
employed in the regular courses offered by the Department,
most of the teaching was done by appointments from outside
and by instructors and professors "borrowed" from other
departments. Despite many frustrations occasioned by sudden
changes in schedules, the program on the whole went well,
and the students proved interested in taking advantage of a
course that offered a combination of writing, reading, and
brief oral presentations. As a result of the program the

Department considered--and experimented briefly--with the idea of incorporating into the regular Freshman English course a little training in oral presentation of material. The following members of the Department participated in varying degrees in the program: Thaler, Emperor, Kirkland, Peck, Soper, Davenport, and Baudin. The best account of the English program is from Thaler's autobiography (pp. 244-45):

> My job as teacher and co-supervisor with John Hodges was challenging and satisfying. It was not difficult . . . to spot first-rate or obviously weak men, and to set them up in five rows of ten men each, each row in charge of a relatively mature or somehow outstanding man to guide and help the rest . . . . I had not taught Freshman English for many years, in fact not since the early 1920's, but all in all, in spite of army rigidity . . . this work was surprisingly rewarding. Our pre-flighters were good men, by and large eager to learn, solid, staunch, and appreciative. For years after the War was over some sent greetings at Christmas time, others looked in at the office when they came to town, and more than a few came back for graduate study with us.

A small graduate program had existed in the Department as early as the turn of the century as evidenced by the listing of a graduate course in the catalogs and the awarding of an occasional master's degree. By the 1920s and 1930s the program for the M.A. was well in place. The four teaching fellows who regularly appear on the roster provided a captive enrollment for the one graduate course offered each year, since their program required teaching two sections of Freshman English, taking the one graduate seminar, and an upper-division course for graduate credit. The graduate seminar rotated among the senior professors, and the enrollment sometimes reached a total of six or seven as an outside student, perhaps a teacher from the public schools, joined the group. A thesis was then required for the degree and an oral examination upon the thesis accompanied by questions on English and American literature. Because there were so few graduate students the burden upon an individual professor was not onerous but rather a welcome relief from the tedium of other chores, especially since several of these M.A. candidates were excellent students who later went on to receive Ph.D.s from northern universities. Because of this well-established M.A. program and the presence in the Department of several Ph.D.s from leading universities, the Department was in a good position to participate in the Ph.D. program to which the University was committing itself for the post-war years.

The most important change--apart from the tremendous increase in enrollments--for the English Department in the post World-War II years was the decision to begin a Ph.D. program and to seek additional staff qualified to contribute to the development of this program. The groundwork, however, for this move was carefully laid during the 1940s, although final approval for the Ph.D. degree in English was not granted until 1946. The University had long had a graduate program in several fields supervised by a Graduate Committee. In 1936, Dr. Fred C. Smith came from Harvard as Dean of the University; he also became Dean of the Graduate School, and thus began the formal structure of what was to be the large and flourishing program of graduate work at the University. Several years earlier the medical units at Memphis had given a Ph.D. degree in several restricted fields. Discussions about possible doctoral programs in several departments on the Knoxville campus came to nothing during the depression because of budgetary restrictions. The adminstration knew that doctoral programs required large sums of money. The first department to receive permission for a Ph.D. was the Department of Chemistry in the fields of physical and organic chemistry. The Graduate Committee recommended this program in the spring of 1943, and the trustees approved it at their summer meeting that year. Thus the University had committed itself to a momentous change from a medium-sized collection of colleges into a University that was to be research-oriented and sought to make itself competitive with the best Universities in the nation and particularly in the South, where several state and private universities in neighboring states already had a significant head start.

The next department to receive permission for the Ph.D. was the Department of Physics. Proximity to Oak Ridge and its personnel and the enormous prestige which the study of physics received from the discovery of the atom bomb, ensured the easy approval of the physics program. But the program in English had to wait for its approval until the fall of 1946 because of determined opposition in ' the College of Liberal Arts. Montgomery's Threshold of a New Day (p. 164) gives no details of the struggle. Green's To Foster Knowledge (p. 198) is brief and cryptic: "The programs of English and physics were supported by secret ballots taken in the university's general faculty, where opponents of the idea lost decisively. The opposition centered on the English proposal, for some of the faculty thought there were already enough unemployed or low-paid English teachers in the country, but the scientists and humanists combined, more or less openly, to push each other's programs through." What I remember and was told is based on two faculty meetings at one of which I was present. At both meetings, Dr. Hofmann, head of the history department, and Dr. Greene, head of political science, spoke at length and repeatedly against the English proposal, and I remember distinctly that one of Greene's arguments was the one which he gives in the above quotation: that there was a sufficient number of English teachers and the University did not need to contribute further to the creation of an "intellectual proletariat"--that phrase I still remember. The day was saved by Dr. W. G. Pollard, a distinguished physicist, who spoke eloquently in behalf of permitting a degree in English, as a program that would please the Department of Physics. Ironically, only a few years later history and political science sought and gained approval for their own Ph.D. programs. How many of their graduates have increased the numbers of the intellectual proletariat I am in no position to say! I can say, however, that many of our Ph.D.s now hold and have held creditable and important positions in colleges and universities, large and small, throughout the land.

The annual reports of the Department record the careful planning a committee of the Department gave to the feasibility of the Ph.D. program. The committee started its work in 1943, submitted a proposal to the University

Committee on the Doctoral Degree the following year, and received approval in principle in 1945. One immediate consequence of these proposals was the appropriation of increased funds for the purchase of much-needed library books. The further account of the Department's Ph.D. program belongs to the next and later chapters of this history.

James D. Hoskins (1870-1960) received B.S. and M.S. degrees from the University of Tennessee in 1891 and 1893, followed by a law degree in 1897. He taught for several years in boys' schools in Knoxville, and after a summer of graduate study at the University of Chicago in 1900, returned to the campus as assistant professor in the new department of history. He taught not only history but also political science, economics, and sociology. He became Dean of the College of Liberal Arts in 1911 with responsibility for student discipline. Eager for power and enjoying its exercise, he became a tough, no-nonsense administrator summarily expelling students for infractions of rules or actions violating his own sense of propriety. Joseph Wood Krutch gave a glimpse of his administrative style as he told of his run-in with Hoskins in 1915 when he was ordered, on pain of expulsion on the eve of his graduation, to cease writing any further articles in the student magazine opposing the prohibition movement. After the death of Ayres in 1919 Hoskins served as acting president for six months until Harcourt Morgan, Dean of the College of Agriculture, was named president. Hoskins then assumed the new post of Dean of the University, but still retained the deanship of Liberal Arts, appointing James Porter as Assistant Dean. Not until 1925 did Hoskins give up the liberal arts post and make Porter Dean.

The presidencies of Dabney and Ayres marked two decades of harmony and absence of internal dissension, but with the coming of Morgan and Hoskins to power trouble began immediately. The summary firing of English Professor George Herbert Clarke was a prelude to the wholesale firing of seven professors in 1923, an action which brought student and faculty unrest, a student underground newspaper, local newspaper attacks on the University and nationwide coverage of the event in the New York Times. An investigation by a committee of the American Association of University

Professors resulted in a lengthy report in their <u>Bulletin,</u>
which gave the University much unfavorable publicity. The
report attacked principally the lack of any system of tenure
and objected to the procedures as open to serious legal and
moral criticism.

Morgan entrusted the administration of the internal
affairs of the University to Hoskins, while he roamed the
state promoting the University among the rural legislators
on whom the University depended for its annual
appropriations. Neither Morgan nor Hoskins was an effective
administrator. As Greene observed: "Hoskins had been a
student in the days when University presidents closely
dominated small faculties, and he seemed never to have come
to terms with the administrative needs of a large
organization." (p. 185) In 1933 Hoskins reached the summit
of his wishes: the presidency of his alma mater when Morgan
accepted a directorship of the Tennessee Valley Authority.
Already in his mid-sixties, Hoskins continued--in the
absence of any retirement system or mandatory retirement
age--until 1946 and the age of seventy-six.

To characterize Hoskins and to be fair to him are
difficult. His life was completely identified with the
University, and no one could have been more loyal and
dedicated to serving its best interests, but his
administrative and personal style alienated most deans,
professors, and students, to say nothing of politicians,
governors, journalists, and potential benefactors. My
assessment may be harsher than that of Greene and others,
but I never had the impression that in his later years--
those of his presidency--he was either admired or liked. He
appears to have adopted a policy of intimidation, threats,
and fear. He threatened students who would not do his
bidding (as we have seen in the Krutch affair) with
expulsion, and faculty with firing. A story that made the
rounds was that when Dr. Hesler, a professor and head of
botany, demurred at accepting the deanship of the College of
Liberal Arts, Hoskins threatened to fire him from the
University. The story has the ring of authenticity, and
Hesler proved to be one of Hoskins' most vocal critics. His
willingness to talk to the University historians,
Montgomery and Greene, has insured that his assessments of
Hoskins' irascibility, cantankerousness, and

unpredictability have been preserved for posterity. Since Hoskins did not leave his account of Hesler we do not have the other side of the story!

Because I made the judgment that the appointment of Burke to a professorship of English in 1909 and in 1923 to the headship of the Department was most unfortunate, I see no reason why I should not be equally frank in making a similar judgment on the appointment of Hoskins as dean and as president. If he had achieved great things for the University such as large endowments and had vigorously pursued the grants from the federal government that neighboring institutions gained, his shortcomings would be condoned. Vanderbilt, Kentucky, Chapel Hill, Duke, and Virginia had able, nationally-known presidents who were leading their institutions to the forefront of universities in the South and gaining the respect of national institutions and (especially) foundations. What admiration and respect could there be for a do-nothing or do-little president?

The charitably minded, even today, after admitting the truth about Hoskins' ineffectiveness and unpleasant social manners, will exclaim: "Oh, but he looked like a college president!" His height and beautiful white hair were, in fact, his greatest assets, and as he walked in the academic procession, any one could feel momentarily proud of the fact that the University had a president who really looked like one!

Teaching Fellows

Early during the presidency of Dr. Dabney someone conceived the idea of having some teaching done inexpensively by employing either advanced undergraduates or graduate students to teach elementary classes. The catalog of 1893-9 announced that four such posts had been created. The recipient would receive $200.00 per year and the remission of fees. Those who sought these appointments addressed their applications to the President, since in those days the President made all decisions as to hiring-- and presumably firing. Since the University seldom had as many as four graduate students in the 1890s these posts were often unfilled, but the idea and the system gradually caught on and continued for about a half century.

By the 1930s the English Department had four teaching fellows. The stipend by then had more than doubled to $450.00 per year or $50.00 per month for nine months for teaching two classes in Freshman English. The teaching fellows later ceased to be teaching fellows and became graduate teaching assistants since it was decided that those with only a bachelor's degree were not mature and seasoned enough to have such responsibility. The change came about in the 1940s in this fashion: a particularly inept and somewhat psychologically maladjusted young woman (whose name shall be unmentioned), chanced to have in her class a very bright and aggressive young woman, who was, unfortunatly for this teaching fellow, the daughter of a university administrator who had the ear of the president. Strong verbal complaints to that high quarter resulted in the fiat from no less a personage than President Hoskins that teaching fellows would no longer teach but would become graduate assistants to senior professors and help them in their more mundane duties. Dr. Hodges had no choice but to follow this order, and that is why we no longer have teaching fellows in the Department of English, and why those with only a bachelor's degree do not normaly teach Freshman English!

The Junior English Exam

The origin of this examination is briefly told in Thaler's Ports and Happy Havens:

> *I managed to suggest and to get adopted as a requirement for graduation in all colleges of our University a simple test in written English for all students at the end of their junior year, to help maintain--or to re-attain, by fresh class or laboratory work--decent standards of writing presumably achieved in Freshman English.*

This requirement, it should be noted, was dropped about 1973. According to Montgomery the faculty in 1928 passed the measure by a vote of 44 to 27. This requirement was not more popular with the English faculty than with the students. The examination worked as follows. On a Saturday afternoon in winter all juniors were required (no exceptions, no excuses) to write a composition on selected topics during a two-hour period. All members of the Department proctored the examination, which was held in rooms scattered over the campus, and later each was given the doubtful pleasure of reading and determining the fates of some sixty juniors. Those who failed were assigned to members of the Department for tutorial work. Each instructor and teaching fellow had from three to six unhappy juniors coming by the office during the spring quarter for conferences, themes, and a final examination. The students thought this to be a conspiracy of the English Department, not the University, and the hapless insructor an instrument of something very like an officer of the Spanish Inquisition. During the 1940s the institution of the Writing Laboratory made it possible for the failed students to attend the laboratory for coaching. The faculty, however, of all ranks regularly read thirty or forty exams each quarter. I cannot speak for all, but I rejoiced when in 1973 the requirement was dropped.

The University of Tennessee Philological Club

A pleasant and scholarly organization closely associated with the English Department was the University of Tennessee Philological Club. On October 10, 1929 members of the language departments of the University met and formed the U. T. Philological Club and elected Dr. Charles Bell Burke, head of the English Department, as president. At its second meeting the Club agreed that its objective should be "to encourage research in philology and literature by the presentation and discussion of papers." After its first year, the Club met monthly for eight meetings during the academic year. The Club lived on until the 1970s when the pressure of other activities and competitive interests and entertainments within the academic community seemed to show that the Club had served its purpose. In a quieter age individuals and groups looked to themselves for opportunities to share congenial interests and the results of their studies. Many papers later saw publication in scholarly journals or became chapters in books. Dr. Hodges, who read the first paper, introduced members of the Club to his studies in Congreve, which culminated in his several books on Congreve published a few years later. The most prolific reader was Professor Alwin Thaler, who presented a paper on Shakespeare almost every year, and whose papers nearly always appeared subsequently in a journal or book. The membership of the Club, however, was not confined to the English Department, but included members of the classical and foreign language departments. For many years a faithful contingent from Maryville and Carson-Newman Colleges attended, notably Dean E. R. Hunter and Dr. Hill Shine of Maryville College. Over the years the Club sponsored lectures by distinguished visiting scholars such as Carleton Brown, David Moore Robinson, the Reverend Dr. Purvis of the Borthwick Institute of York, and John Crow of the University of London. The Club may be viewed as a tribute to the determination of a small group of dedicated scholars to encourage study and writing in the humanities in the face of limited and often non-existent institutional funds and support.

Note: *A short history was written by Kenneth Curry, A Register of Papers, The University of Tennessee Philological Club, The University of Tennessee Record, 61 (1958), No. 4 (July). The minute-books of the Club are on deposit in Special Collections, University Library.*

CHAPTER VI

POST-WAR GROWTH: THE HODGES YEARS: 1945-1962

The end of the war found the Department reduced in size to a professorial staff of six: three full professors, two associates, and one assistant. Of the twenty-seven instructors at the end of the first post-war year (1945-46) nineteen were added during the winter and spring terms. The tremendous influx of students began in the fall and can be detected in the rise in enrollments in Freshman English from the spring quarter of 1945 when 481 were enrolled to the fall quarter of 1945 with 887. The figures, however, for the following year--the fall of 1946--are even more staggering: 3,339. These enrollment pressures forced the adminstration to authorize additional staff, and during 1946-47 two full professors and two assistant professors were hired, not to mention thirty-five instructors. How the Department and the University coped with this terrific influx I do not know, but in some way all responded to the best of their abilities, and the students proved to be serious, hard-working, and eager to make up for lost time. This wave of new students, however, receded as enrollment in the freshman course dropped by almost one half to 1,825 in the fall of 1947. The sophomore courses increased from 1,117 to 1,493. The Department, with administrative approval, continued to add staff during 1947-48: two associate professors, five assistant professors, and nine instructors. These additions were offset by the resignation of nineteen instructors, mostly from those employed during the emergency of 1946.

The post-war years introduced a whole new era for the Department and the University. President C. E. Brehm, the former Dean of Agricultural Extension, assumed the presidency following the retirement of President Hoskins. Brehm recognized the need for a change in administrative procedures necessary for a rapidly growing mega-University to be operated by a system of delegation of powers. Brehm's personal style and poor speaking ability led to some grumbling by the faculty, but those who had business dealings with him reported that he was rational and agreeable in contrast to his predecessor. His experience in the extension program provided him with excellent political

[67]

contacts so that he knew how to advance the interests of the institution in legislative circles, with governors and state officials. He was able--an important service--to spare the University from the witch-hunts of the 1950s by zealous legislators who may have sought to look for subversion and assorted forms of immorality on state college campuses. By contrast, presidents of several other state universities were not so successful.

Although the presidency changed in 1945, the two administrative officers most directly affecting the Department remained: Deans Smith and Hesler. Dean of the University Fred C. Smith (later Vice-President) remained in his post and in addition became the Dean of the Graduate School. Hesler, the Dean of Liberal Arts, was to remain in that post until 1958. Smith, so the story went, was bitterly disappointed at being passed over for the presidency, which he thought had been implicitly promised him when he came to the University ten years previously from Harvard. Consequently, he may not have had as much influence over final decisions--such as the allocation of the University general funds--as his position might imply. A kindly and friendly man, Smith was perceived by the faculty to have their interests at heart. As chairman of the Graduate Committee he had approved in principle the Ph.D. proposal from the Department in 1944. My impression is that he was essentially sympathetic and supportive of the interests of the graduate programs including that of English.

The last chapter told the story of the procedures by which the Department gained approval for its Ph.D. The English Ph.D. program, once it had been approved, received the careful attention of the entire English professorial staff. The decision was to proceed carefully in the admission of students for the degree, but not to neglect the M.A. program which was already on a sound footing. The enrollment in the graduate programs expanded slowly. The first Ph.D. was awarded in 1950 to Edward C. McAleer, whose dissertation on Browning under the direction of Knickerbocker was later published as a book. The second Ph.D. in 1952--and the first awarded by the University to a woman--was to Minnie Cate Morrell, whose dissertation on medieval English psalters under the direction of Parker was also published in book form. Almost every year thereafter one to three others received a Ph.D. By 1961-62 the graduate enrollment had soared to 70, a marked increase from the 50 of the previous year. In that same year the University received a generous allotment of NDEA Fellowships of which the Graduate School awarded three five-year fellowships to the Department. A roster of the Ph.D.s awarded by the Department forms one of the appendices to this history.

The requirements for the Ph.D. in English did not differ markedly from those in other graduate schools of the day. Two foreign languages (French and German), comprehensive written examinations covering English and American literature, and twenty-seven courses (81 quarter hours) beyond the B.A. were the basic requirements. The courses were to include Old and Middle English and language, and nine hours of graduate work in a field outside the English Department. Most courses were in graduate seminars, but a limited number could be in certain upper-division courses taken for graduate credit. To those familiar with graduate programs at American universities the requirements will have a familiar ring. The Tennessee Ph.D. program, although liberalized in some directions over the years, has never been revolutionary. Indeed, the position of the Department has been that most demands for radical change-- such as those that questioned the "relevance" of Chaucer, Milton, Wordsworth in favor of current writing and journalism--should be resisted, and that any change should be adopted only after thoughtful consideration.

The increased enrollments at the University, the improved financial support from state and federal governments, and a new administration gave the Department the opportunity to advance rapidly and to begin to realize its long dormant potential. The University's approval of the Ph.D. program in English was the catalyst for the amazing transformation of a small, sleepy Department which had lacked institutional support for its work into a lively, expanding Department. The one individual who was largely responsible for this transformation was Dr. John Hodges, who had been planning for this post-war change with his colleagues during the difficult years of the war. Where others in the University had been pessimistic and defeatist,

Dr. Hodges was positive and hopeful and confident that, given the opportunity, the Department would justify his faith.   He recognized the importance of staffing the Department with able persons including young men who had the potential for growth.   Within three years (1946-48) he employed Kenneth Knickerbocker and Richard B. Davis as full professors, John L. Lievsay as Associate Professor, and Percy G. Adams, Robert Daniel, John Hansen, and F. DeWolfe Miller as assistant professors.   Three of these held Ph.D.s from Yale, two from Virginia, and one each from Texas and Washington.   A year later he employed Nathalia Wright, another Yale Ph.D., and the first woman to be assistant professor since the resignation of Miss Skeffington in 1905. Most of these remained until their retirement, while others served many years before departing for Duke (Lievsay) and Kenyon (Daniel).   All these people justified his faith in them and contributed their several abilities and talents to the Department, the University, and the profession.   In view of the fact that the post-war years were a sellers' and not a buyers' market, this achievement is all the more notable as other institutions, many with more money and some, alas, with more glamor, tradition, and ivy-covered walls, were also in the competition for promising young professionals. Four holdovers from "before the war" were Paul Soper, Kenneth Curry, Charles Mangam, and Bain Stewart, who although officially chosen by Dr. Burke, were certainly choices about which Hodges had considerable influence. Mangam left after a few years to become department head at Tennessee Tech and later at the University of Tennessee at Martin;   the   others   remained   at   the   University   until retirement.

The speech and theatre programs within the Department enjoyed a consistent, healthy growth and paralleled the increased University enrollments as well as an increasing acceptance of theatre by the University and Knoxville community.   During these years very few touring companies offered live theatre in Knoxville, so that the U. T. Playhouse was able to fill a market niche.   By 1952 the erection of Carousel Theatre made possible year-round presentation of plays directed by Professors Soper, Fields, and Green with casts composed of students and Knoxvillians; many of the latter had had both training in schools of drama

and professional stage experience.   In addition to the
presentation of plays for the town-and-gown audience, the
Department inaugurated several courses designed to train
students to direct plays, coach actors, and to develop the
necessary technical "back-stage" knowledge needed to direct
and produce plays.   Several students from this program
became directors of plays in high schools and community
theatres.   A few student actors later went on to
professional careers in acting such as John Cullum, David
Keith, Bette Henritze, Colin Wilcox, and Brandon Maggart.

After the opening of Carousel Theatre the program
advanced rapidly.   By 1960 the U. T. Playhouse was producing
ten plays a session: five during the summer and five during
the winter plus a group of plays for Children's Theatre.
The plays had runs from one to two weeks.   A few titles from
the 1960-61 season give a sample of the variety and quality
of the plays offered the community: Rattigan's <u>Separate
Tables</u>, Miller's <u>Death of a Salesman</u>, Rodgers' and Hart's
musical <u>Pal Joey</u>, Shaw's <u>Candida</u>, and Chekhov's <u>Uncle
Vanya</u>.

Four small programs in the Department during the pre-
war and immediate post-war years developed into important
programs within the Department or became separate entities
and moved outside the Department.   These four were: radio-
television; speech correction; English for foreign students;
and creative writing.

Radio grew from a one-year course in 1947 taught by
instructors in speech to several courses, and was greatly
helped by the establishment of the University's FM Station
WUOT, which offered opportunities for practical experience
to the students.   Radio, in turn, expanded to include
television with Kenneth Wright and Frank Lester providing
leadership for this work.   Ultimately radio and television
left the Department to become units in the College of
Communications.

Speech correction had a modest beginning before the war
when an instructor, Charles Ranous, helped three or four
students in speech classes with their speech difficulties.
In 1947-48 the Department established a Speech Clinic to
help students with speech defects and placed Arthur L.
Kaltenborn, Jr., an instructor in speech, who was also a
speech   therapist,   in   charge.   In   1959   Dr.   Bernard

Silverstein, a lecturer in the Department, taught speech correction, but the whole program in speech correction was soon absorbed into the Department of Audiology and Speech Pathology and in close association with the East Tennessee Hearing and Speech Center, which occupied new and specially designed and equipped facilities in a building at the corner of Yale Avenue and Stadium Drive.

The first attempt of the Department to provide help for students at the University for whom English was a second language began in 1948 when a special course in English was designated for foreign students. It was hoped that after spending the first two quarters of Freshman English in this course they would be able to join a regular class of Freshman English for the third quarter. The expansion of this work to the large size of the present belongs to the next chapter of this history where a description will be included.

Creative writing--fiction, poetry, plays, the familiar essay--has only recently become a prominent activity of the Department. We have already noted how students, with the encouragement and participation of the faculty banded together and published their writings in a University Magazine. Two interesting and creditable efforts from the 1840s and 1890s have already been described. Special Collections contains the files of these as well as several other student literary publications. An ambitious "humor" magazine, more distinguished for its art work than its literary distinction, appeared in the 1920s. These bursts of creative activity seem to be spontaneous and come about because a group of like-minded and talented individuals are in the same place at the same time. It does not seem to arise from official sponsorship or an officially inaugurated program. Although no such group at Tennessee ever emerged to rival the Fugitives at Vanderbilt in the 1920s, that group, it must be noted, arose from a handful of talented young men (assisted by a wealthy Nashville litterateur who financed their magazine) and not from formal sponsorship by Vanderbilt or its English department.

In the 1930s the Department initiated a course in writing of fiction, which always attracted a small group of would-be writers, and was taught by members of the Department who had enjoyed some success in writing and

publishing fiction: Maurice Baudin, Jr., in the early
1940s; C. P. Lee, author of several novels, and Robert
Daniel. Daniel encouraged two undergraduate students who
wrote (and continue to write) novels that have had wide
acclaim and recognition: David (then known as Jerry) Madden
and Cormac McCarthy (then know as Charles J. McCarthy, Jr.).
In 1958 the Ingram-Merrill Foundation gave the Department a
one-year grant of $250.00 for the encouragement of creative
writing among students. During the winter and spring terms
of 1959 the award was given to Charles J. McCarthy, Jr., on
the basis of his work in English 345 (the Writing of
Fiction) and other courses in English. Professor Daniel was
then the teacher of the course.

From time to time play-writing contests have been held
with the winning plays receiving dramatic presentation on
the campus. Donors provided small cash prizes for these,
and a few small endowments have also provided prizes for the
writing of poetry, fiction, and essays. In some years,
however, there were no contestants as interest in writing
waxed or waned.

The expanded program in creative writing had to await
the arrival of Robert Drake in 1965 and Jon Manchip White in
1977, the latter of whom was to inaugurate a more extensive
program leading to a master's degree.

The Library has always been essential to the proper
conduct of any program in English Studies--Dr. John Bell
Henneman in the 1890s called the Library "the workshop of
the English student." The annual reports of the Department
(which begin in 1936-37) repeat with monotonous regularity
the need for adequate support for the Library. The planning
for the Ph.D. program insured that the funds, when
available, came to the Department in due course. All
members of the Department were united in this objective,
and--to look ahead in this narrative--Dr. Hodges after his
retirement in 1962 devoted his last years to procuring gifts
for the Library by active solicitation of donors and
collectors of books.

After 1945 the annual reports devoted a section on the
progress that the Library was making by listing a few
notable acquisitions during the year. Special
appropriations from the administration enabled the
Department to proceed vigorously and with the active

cooperation of the acquisitions librarian, Miss Branch. For
many years Dr. Thaler had been in charge of book orders from
the Department, but when he assumed the directorship of the
Department's graduate program, he relinquished the duty of
book acquisitions to me, a post which I held with pleasure
for many years. The arrival of Richard B. Davis in 1948
resulted in the growth and strengthening of the section on
American literature (especially in his field of colonial
Southern literature and history). For many years the two
of us worked harmoniously and enjoyed the triumphs of
acquiring hundreds of desirable items. In those days
important books and serials were available (by careful
scrutiny of booksellers' catalogs) at prices ridiculously
low by present-day standards. Two fields which we sought
especially to build were the neglected periods of American
and British literature and runs of American and British
periodicals of those centuries. As a result of this effort
the Library has a respectable collection of general
antiquarian and literary periodicals from the eighteenth
century to the present day. The professors in the
Department made a systematic effort to form complete
collections of not only well-known authors but also of
secondary authors. The work of building a library is, of
course, never done, but in those years the foundations were
laid for the excellent collection in the fields in which the
Department has its strengths.

The next chapter will describe the successful post-
retirement efforts of Dr. Hodges to assist in the Library's
development program and will look forward to the erection
and dedication of the John C. Hodges Undergraduate Library
in 1969. The final recognition of Dr. Hodges' work in
behalf of the Library (and, I add, that of the Department!)
was to come in 1987 when the Undergraduate and Main Library
were housed together in the magnificent new John C. Hodges
Library.

The great influx of students in the mid-1940s and the
inauguration of the Ph.D. program brought tremendous growth
in numbers of students and staff to the Department. But the
great wave receded almost as quickly as it had advanced.
The demand for a large number of sections--and instructors--
for the freshman-sophomore courses diminished rapidly. The
decrease in the size of the Department from a total of 50 in

1947-48 to a low of 18 plus 12 part-time instructors was truly drastic. This reduction in enrollment placed a severe burden on the administration at all levels with the result that the early and mid-fifties were a difficult period. Addition of staff at the level of assistant, associate, and full professor came to an abrupt halt, and exacted its toll on faculty morale, as promotions and raises, which had been more freely distributed in the forties, now dropped to a trickle. Those which came were usually thought of as too little and too late.

Despite many discouraging aspects of the fifties the Department and individuals within it were making reputations for themselves--and the University--by their publications and the award of national fellowships from government and private foundations. The following list for the years 1945-1961 is impressive:

1953-54 Richard B. Davis, Fulbright Professorship to the University of Oslo, Norway

John L. Lievsay, Fulbright Research Fellowship to Italy

Nathalia Wright, Guggenheim Fellowship for study in Washington, D.C. and Italy

1954-55 Robert Daniel, Fulbright Lectureship to Greece

John Hansen, Ford Faculty Fellowship to Columbia University

1955-56 C. P. Lee, Fulbright Professorship at the University of Athens, Greece

1959 Nathalia Wright, American Association of University Women Fellowship

1961 Richard B. Davis, Guggenheim Fellowship, Spring, 1961

1960-61   Durant Da Ponte, Fulbright Lectureship to the
          University of Salamanca, Spain

The last decade of the Hodges administration marked the presence in the Department of several young instructors, who later distinguished themselves: Alan Markman (1953-36) left for the University of Pittsburgh, where he later became Director of Graduate Study before his untimely death; O. B. Hardison (1954-56) became the Director of the Folger Shakespeare Library; John B. Vickery (1954-56), who has published extensively in the area of myth and literature, is Professor of English at the University of California, Riverside; James L. Allen (1954-56), who returned to the Department in 1976-77 as a visiting professor from his post at the University of Hawaii; Raymond C. Sutherland (1953-57, a Ph.D. from Kentucky, went to Georgia State University at Atlanta; Madison P. Jones (1955-56), who is well known for his novels with a Southern setting. Thomas Wheeler, who has written extensively on Renaissance literature, joined the department in 1955 and is now the senior member of the professorial staff in length of service.

In 1960 Hodges appointed Eric Stockton, a Harvard Ph.D. and author of a book on John Gower, to replace Holger Nygard, who had gone to Duke. In 1960 he also appointed Stephen A. Mooney, Jr., an able poet and writer, who later went to the University of Tennessee at Martin, where he established the Tennessee Poetry Press. In 1961 Thomas P. Cooke, with a degree from Yale, replaced Russell Green. Cooke later left Tennessee for the University of South Carolina, but returned to the University as head of the Department of Speech and Theatre in 1987. Three other appointments were made in 1961: John D. Tinkler, a Ph.D. from Stanford, who went to the University of Tennessee, Chattanooga, in 1967; George T. Wright, a Ph.D. from California at Berkeley and a talented twentieth-century scholar, who went to the University of Minnesota in 1968; and, finally, Jack E. Reese, a Ph.D. from Kentucky, who moved to the Graduate School as assistant dean in 1964, and finally became chancellor of the University of Tennessee, Knoxville, a post which he now holds. Hodges' final appointment appears to have been that of Norman J. Sanders

(Ph.D., Shakespeare Institute, Stratford-on-Avon) whose appointment was effective September 1, 1962, just one day after Hodges' official retirement date of August 31, 1962.

The tremendous growth of the Department after 1945 made it necessary to organize the Department more elaborately. In the 1920s and 1930s a simple organization had sufficed: Hodges had responsibility for the Freshman English program; Thaler for the Sophomore, and Emperor for Public Speaking. The four or five with professorial rank constituted The Department Council. The system of organization that developed with changing conditions was as follows:

The chairman of Freshman English managed the large staff of instructors and teaching assistants responsible for over one hundred sections of Freshman English. One or two senior instructors were given reduced teaching loads in order to advise new, beginning instructors. An ad hoc committee reviewed student folders in order to provide a basis for offering constructive advice to new assistant professors, instructors, and teaching assistants. In earlier and simpler days, Dr. Hodges had easily done this task in an afternoon!

The chairman of the Graduate Program supervised all phases of the graduate work, prepared a brochure describing the requirements of the degree, handled the correspondence and applications for admission, selected the graduate and teaching assistants, and recipients of scholarships. As the program grew the chairman was soon assisted by one or two co-chairmen, who with the head of the Department and usually the chairman of Freshman English constituted a graduate committee of five which met weekly to make plans and decisions.

As the options for Sophomore English developed, a chairman for each one of the options became responsible for each sequence: the traditional survey of English literature, the one-quarter course in American literature, and the three-quarter sequence of world literature.

The director of the English Writing Laboratory managed a small staff of instructors who tutored students with deficiencies in English.

The director of English for Foreign Students was responsible for the program, the texts, and the method of instruction. He prepared and graded the qualifying examinations, and, generally, related this phase of English instruction to the University's commitment to students for whom English was a second language.

The chairman of upper-division English courses handled all problems connected with these courses, as well as the majors and minors. This chairman often doubled as chairman of one of the Sophomore English courses.

As long as the Speech and Theatre programs were in the Department they too had separate chairmen for their courses and staff.

The director of Scheduling had the complicated, and unenviable, task of setting up the weekly schedule for each staff member within the constraints of time and available classroom space--to say nothing of coping with privileges of seniority and the artistic temperament.

The director of Sectioning with his assistants (often dozens) had the difficult task of placing students in various sections of Freshman and Sophomore English at the beginning of registration each quarter. In the last few years the introduction of computer registration has greatly eased this burden.

The coordinator for Library Acquisitions acts as a liaison between the Department and the Acquisitions Department of the Library. The coordinator of Textbook Purchases processes the requests for textbooks from the Department to the University Bookstore.

The University has heads, not chairmen (or chairpersons). Until John Fisher became the head in 1976, and effected a sweeping organizational restructuring, the head was responsible for the entire program including the hiring of staff, assignment of courses and departmental chores, and the ticklish matter of salary adjustments. In the last matter the head might or might not consult one or two senior professors. In other matters the full professors met somewhat irregularly and served as an advisory committee to the head on the business at hand. Although the procedure is seemingly quite undemocratic, it actually worked in a democratic way. On more than one occasion the head acceded to the wishes of the majority of the full professors even when the action went against his own wish or preference. The head, however, was by no means the final arbiter since the dean of the college and others in the academic

hierarchy, including the presidents and the trustees, could
(and sometime did) overrule the recommendations of a
departmental head.

Until his retirement in 1958 Dean of Liberal Arts L. R.
Hesler played a key role in the development of the English
program, but a role difficult to assess. Departments always
vie with each other for a share in the limited funds which
the University allots each college. Hesler appeared to be
more sympathetic towards the sciences than to the
humanities, but as the conscientious person which he was, he
certainly granted many of the English requests, or the
Department could not have made the great strides which it
did during the post-war years. Hodges, ever tactful, was
also ever patient, and knew that what he did not get in one
year he might obtain in another. I did not know at the
time, however, that one of the prices he paid for smooth and
tranquil relations with deans and presidents was a
willingness to take the blame personally for unpopular
actions or rejections by the dean and president. Hesler
and Hodges were always friendly, but they were of opposing
temperaments: where Hodges was hopeful and optimistic,
Hesler was pessimistic, seeing objections to any thing new,
and finding a ready excuse for postponement with the
assertion that, alas, there was no money. Despite his
somewhat dour temperament, Hesler was affable, talkative,
and approachable. A specialist in the study of mushrooms,
he was, I think, happier doing botanical research than in
coping with the trials and tribulations of a deanship. He
valued advanced study and research, and I am sure regretted
that the college could not afford more aid to the staff. He
provoked both strong loyalties and strong antipathies, and I
remember that a few members of the faculty openly said they
feared to cross him. But the final verdict has to be that
during a difficult quarter century Hesler stood for high
academic standards and respect for learning and scholarship
in a collegiate atmosphere that all too often seemed to
place a higher value on popularity, "inspirational"
teaching, and winning athletic teams.

The following sketches of former faculty members are
intended as tributes to those in the Department who deserve
honor and remembrance.

Roscoe E. Parker (1890-1984) came to the Department in 1927 as Associate Professor (promoted to Professor in 1934) and the Department's medievalist. A North Carolinian, Parker graduated from the University of North Carolina at Chapel Hill, where he was a pupil of Edwin Greenlaw. He taught in the public schools of North Carolina until World War I in which he served achieving the rank of captain. He received an M.A. from the University of Minnesota under the tutelage of Carleton Browne, taught a year at Drake University, and then did graduate study at the University of California at Berkeley from which he received a Ph.D. From there he came to Tennessee. His dissertation on the Middle English stanzaic versions of the life of Saint Anne was published by the Early English Text Society in 1928. Parker taught the courses in medieval literature, the history of the language, and also a course in advanced composition. He also introduced and organized an advanced course, The Bible as Literature. Because of his experience as a high-school teacher he was well qualified to teach the course in the teaching of English, which at that time was taught in the Department and not in the College of Education to which it was later transferred. The result of his teaching the course in advanced composition was a book Advanced Composition, co-authored with Harry Robbins of Lehigh, which went into several editions after its first publication in 1933. His book, The Principles and Practice of Teaching English, appeared in 1937 under the imprint of Prentice-Hall.

For many years Parker was active in the Southern Association of Schools and Colleges and organized and directed a series of work conferences for educators during the summer. The results of these conferences appeared in his edition of Studies of Higher Education in the South published in 1946 by the Committee on Work conferences. As a consequence of this work with the Southern Association he became well acquainted with many deans, presidents, and heads of foundations. The only name I remember in particular was that of Oliver Carmichael, variously chancellor of Vanderbilt and head of the Carnegie Foundation. On more than one occasion he was offered a deanship at well-known universities, but he preferred teaching to administration. Despite his respectable list of publications and his important connections in the educational world Parker was a prophet who lacked honor in his own department and university. He once remarked to me that he had more influence in the Southern Association than in the Department of English. The failure to use his very considerable talents and level-headed administrative skills was a loss to all concerned. Because of this lack of support Parker retired at sixty-five in 1956. An able man with countless friends in the University and in the academic world, he certainly received shabby treatment from the University for reasons I do not know, but I suspect it was due to Dean Hesler, who could be an implacable foe.

Both Dr. Parker and his wife Katharine had an unusually wide circle of friends, and did much to improve the social life of the Department. They entertained all the members of the Department once a year, especially the graduate students and younger members of the Department, with whom they established a congenial rapport. The Parkers, more than most members of the faculty, gave meaning to the Southern phrase "gracious living" and generously shared their hospitality with their friends. I was fortunate to earn their special friendship, which I happily enjoyed and valued for some forty years. After their retirement to Fort Myers Beach, Florida, they received a steady stream of visitors who made the special trip to that remote outpost to pay their respects and enjoy their good and lively company.

Miss Mamie C. Johnston joined the English Department in 1920 with the rank of assistant professor, but for some unexplained reason she was demoted the following year to instructor, a rank which she retained until her retirement in 1949. Miss Johnston had completed most or all of the course work for a Ph.D. at the University of Chicago, but an accident which resulted in a broken hip and required her to use crutches for the rest of her life presumably made it impossible for her to fulfill the final

requirements for the degree. Miss Johnston as the senior instructor in the Department was admired by all her colleagues and was widely recognized as an excellent teacher of sophomore and freshman English as students sought admission to her sections rather than to those of the young Ph.D.s from Yale and Harvard! A graduate of Tusculum College and with M.A.s from Tusculum and the University of Tennessee, Miss Johnston had a cheerful disposition and was a most agreeable and pleasant conversationalist at receptions and dinners.
As I look back I realize that she was a strong and courageous person. If she had any resentment at the way in which her years of competent and faithful service went unrewarded, she never showed any such feelings. Dr. Hodges did what he could to make things easy for her by giving her the schedule she requested and providing her with the office nearest the front door and an adjacent classroom to meet her classes. Her situation is almost a textbook (or classic) example of the unfortunate plight of an able, intelligent woman in the academic world of the 1920s, 1930s, and 1940s. I conclude this sketch by quoting a statement given me by one of her students, David Harkness, who thought her one of the best teachers he had during his four years at the University:

I was fortunate to have Miss Mamie for the sophomore survey course in English and American literature. She brought to her classes a genuine love of the subject and a true interest in her students as individuals. I looked forward to a conference with her and each time I came away with a warm and happy feeling. She made Wordsworth and Coleridge come alive with her pictures and accounts of her visit to the Lake District. When I was teaching English in high school I often thought of her and realized that she had provided inspiration for which I was truly grateful.

John Bernard Emperor (1902-1945) joined the Department in 1929. Emperor took charge of the program in public speaking which had existed as a one-year course taught almost every year by a different instructor. His specialty in English literature was the eighteenth century, and he taught the first graduate course in that field in 1941. Grounded in Latin and Greek, Emperor developed the one-year course in comparative literature which, in addition to the quarter course in classical literature, had two other quarters in western European literature. He can thus be said to be the founder of the programs in public speaking and comparative literature, now far expanded beyond their modest beginnings. Emperor was a dynamic, even flamboyant, personality, and a lively and popular classroom instructor. He was much given to what I call sesquipedalian humor. One example will illustrate: when the University and Department were threatened by a loss of students, Emperor's comment was: "I doubt that any of us will be kept around as elegant supernumeraries." Emperor was a particular favorite of the Thalers, Hodgeses, and Heslers, and was on excellent terms with the Parkers and Burkes. I gradually came to know him well, and we became the best of friends as I enjoyed his form of humor and was amused by his skilful employment of Irish blarney. From his modest salary he saved money and regularly placed his savings in stocks (he was a consistent reader of the Financial World). The result was that after his early death in 1945 at the age of forty-three (followed soon after by that of his wife) the Department received from his estate its first endowment: twenty-seven thousand dollars. The income from this small sum enabled the Department to do many worthwhile things such as providing small subventions for book publication by the staff. Emperor's fatal illness was the consequence of a childhood attack of rheumatic fever which left him with a weakened heart. I consider his untimely death a great loss to the students and faculty of the University and to his many friends. An idea of the affection in which he was held by many in the Department can be attested by one small fact: Dr. Hodges for many years kept two photographs in his office: one of J. Douglas Bruce; the other, John Bernard Emperor.

Alwin Thaler (1891-1977) as scholar and writer is a worthy follower of the tradition of Kent, Henneman, Bruce, and Clarke in having more than a local and parochial reputation. His Shakespeare's Silences (1928) established him in the front rank of Shakespearean scholars. He regularly read papers at the annual meetings of the Modern Language Association, published ten articles in PMLA, and once chaired the important Shakespeare section of MLA. When he did not teach in the summer term at Tennessee, he taught in the summer at Harvard and Texas. In 1925-26 he was a visiting professor at Stanford University; in 1952, at Chapel Hill; and after his retirement in 1961 he spent two happy years as emeritus visiting professor at Emory University. Thaler was the first member of the department to receive a Guggenheim Fellowship, which enabled him to spend fifteen months (1929-30) in England. I cite these facts to remind those who knew him, as well as those who joined the department later, of the recognition and achievement he received. A significant number of his former students have written me to speak of their happy and grateful recollections of their association with him at the University.

Dr. Thaler was a pleasant person to meet and to know, and he enjoyed the company of like-minded friends, especially those he had known for many years. He and Mrs. Thaler were exceptionally hospitable, entertaining their colleagues and graduate students in their home at frequent intervals. I was a guest at least once a year until Mrs. Thaler's illness made entertaining no longer possible. The best way to discover the Thalerian essence is by reading--or skipping about--in his Ports and Happy Havens, a 297-page autobiography which he wrote at eighty.

The last years of Dr. Thaler were sad as he outlived all his family and his old friend and colleague John Hodges. A reader of this autobiography is impressed by his happy home life, his devotion to his family, and his pride in the achievements of his two sons. The older, Richard (Harvard M.D.) practiced medicine in Boston and died at fifty. The younger, Roderick (Harvard Ph.D.) was a professor of history at Bishop's University in Canada and died in his mid-forties. Mrs. Thaler died after a series of strokes. These losses left him quite alone in his home near the University on Terrace Avenue until his death in his eighty-seventh year.

To speak of Dr. John C. Hodges is to speak of the history and development of the Department for approximately forty years. Employed by Bruce in 1921, Hodges quickly made himself useful by taking over the moribund program of Freshman English which Burke had mismanaged to the displeasure of Dean Hoskins and by making it acceptable to the several colleges whose students were required to take the course. He designed a system of not only the writing of papers but also of seeing that papers were corrected and revised. The students kept their papers in a folder, and at the end of the quarter turned in their folders with the corrected papers. Instructors in the course were expected to have two conferences with each student and go over the papers with the student to determine their weaknesses and recommend ways of improving the compositions. The program was as demanding of the instructors as of the students. At one time, changed later, two themes per week were written: one in class; another, out of class. In order to provide guidance to the changing corps of instructors and teaching fellows, Hodges conducted weekly staff meetings. In those leisurely days no English classes were hald at 11:00 a.m. on Tuesdays, Thursdays, and Saturdays so that Tuesdays were regularly pre-empted for these staff meetings. In those days attendance was expected, and, since the staff was relatively small, any absence was conspicuous. Because the instructors and fellows came from a large cross-section of the nation, it seemed reasonable that the marking of the papers by this diverse group would exhibit a fair picture of what freshman instructors everywhere

considered important. Since the folders of the
students were kept for several years, these papers
could be analyzed and the results tabulated. Hodges
concluded that most handbooks of composition included
much materal that was ignored and irrelevant to the
teaching of composition. Hence he evolved the concept
of the Harbrace Handbook of English, which sought to
reduce and simplify the points of grammar, punctuation,
and sentence structure that were the essentials of any
course in Freshman English. The Harbrace Handbook
appeared in 1941, twenty years after Hodges' arrival
at the University. I have heard that students (work-
study students) did much of the statistical tabulation
of the folders. Hodges, however, kept an eye on what
new instructors were doing, and he regularly reviewed
the folders--a custom that has continued to the present
day--as a way of helping beginning instructors and
ensuring uniformity of standards.

Because the Department existed in a steadily
growing University it was important that the required
freshman and sophomore courses give satisfaction to
their constituents. I hasten to say, however, that in
those happy far-off days the constituents were not the
students who took the courses, but the professorial
staffs of the several colleges who prescribed the
course requirements for their students. Hodges was in
the habit of explaining the courses from time to time
either to the faculty of separate colleges or to a
committee of a college looking into the nooks and
crannies of the curriculum.

Hodges had been at the University only a little
over two years before the death of James Douglas Bruce
created a vacancy at the professorial level. He
recommended his old Harvard friend, Alwin Thaler, then
an assistant professor at the University of California
at Berkeley, who arrived in the fall of 1923, and the
two can be said to have provided the direction and
leadership of the Department for the next several
decades. They were both able scholars, effective
teachers, and eager to improve the program in English.
Furthermore, both were tactful and persuasive in
promoting their programs to those in the

administration and within the Department.

I may use the personal pronoun too often in this history, but when I come to persons and events of which I have personal knowledge, I think such is the proper procedure. I believe that John Hodges was one of the most tactful persons I have ever known. He was expert in the use of the soft answer that turns away, if not always wrath, perhaps irritation, disappointment, or dissatisfaction. I have even found myself--after long observation of his skill in such situations--asking myself how Dr. Hodges would handle this irate student, fussy colleague, or annoying telephone caller. I have been asked by new members of the Department how some of these former professors were. I found it easy to say something of Burke, Thaler, Parker, and Emperor, but I find it more difficult to make a statement about Dr. Hodges as he was a more complex and many-sided person. As far as I was concerned--from the first time I met him until the last time some thirty-two years later--he was unfailingly polite and considerate. He was a kindly man who wished to do what he could to make the lives of those in the Department pleasant. On several occasions he showed this kindness and consideration for me; however, in many ways he was severely limited by restrictions placed upon him by the dean of the college, the dean of the university, and the president. After a few years I discovered that he was taking the blame for actions that were rightly the fault of a dean or president. As a result, some people in the Department held hard feelings towards him when he was only protecting the administration. I think he was unfair to himself in this respect. A simple example of what I mean can be found in my account of the teaching fellows in which he protected President Hoskins.

His greatest skill lay in his recruitment of an able staff, so that in some ways the Department represented for twenty-five years after his retirement his lengthened shadow. And the final contribution to the department and to the University was his munificent establishment of the Hodges Better English Fund, an account of which I give elsehwere in this history. The

University has fittingly honored him by its naming and dedication of the magnificent new John C. Hodges Library in his honor.

Tennessee Studies in Literature

Tennessee Studies in Literature, founded in 1957 by Professor Alwin Thaler, recently published its thirtieth volume. Its first volume proclaimed it to be "an annual journal of literary scholarship and criticism" with a new volume promised each year. This journal has published many notable articles and has provided a forum for articles by members of the Tennessee English Department, and, very happily, the first publication for many of the Department's former graduate students. As the journal became known, outstanding scholars sent in contributions especially if they were writing upon a Southern or Tennessee topic. In the first volume eight of the ten articles were by University faculty with Tennessee-oriented topics represented by da Ponte's "Tennessee's Tennessee Williams" and Daniel's "The Nashville Critics." By the tenth volume only four of the fourteen articles were by University of Tennessee authors with two of the four by former graduate students. A special number appeared in 1961 as *Studies in Honor of John C. Hodges and Alwin Thaler* to mark their retirement by essays from colleagues and former students. The miscellaneous character of the journal gradually changed as volumes were devoted to particular topics such as medieval studies (1966 and 1985). With volume 27 (1984) the series adopted a new format: each issue was to deal with a specific theme, period, genre, for which the editor invited contributions from leading scholars in the field, and departing from the strict format of an annual series, a volume was to be published only when ready. The resulting change has been to give *TSL* more of a national or international flavor.

Restoration: Studies in English Literary Culture: 1660-1700

Jack M. Armistead of the English Department conceived the idea of a news letter that would inform scholars in the field of Restoration studies, cultural as well as literary, of articles, books, and projects as these works appeared or were conceived. This was in 1975, and in 1977, with the financial assistance of the John C. Hodges Better English Fund, the first number appeared in the spring. Armistead's co-editor was David Vieth, and the first three issues were largely written by them, with notices of forthcoming meetings, reports on past meetings, announcements, and queries. By 1978 the journal had expanded to include articles on topics of literary and general culture of the Restoration period. Armistead, the editor, has the assistance of a board of internationally known scholars, members of which referee the articles submitted. The articles in Restoration, now in its eleventh year, tend to be those that imply familiarity with the social and intellectual climate which informs the literary works under discussion.

A Word on University Salaries

Before 1920 deans were paid between $3,200.00 and $5,000.00; professors $2,100.00 and $3,000.00; associate professors, $1,400.00 and $2,100.00; assistant professors, $800.00 and $1,600.00. By 1929 the prosperity of the 1920s had increased the level somewhat; deans $4,700.00 and $6,750; professors, $3,500.00 and $4,200; associate professors, $2,700.00 and $3,500; assistant professors, $2,000.00 and $2,600; and the lowly instructor from $1,500.00 to $2,000.00. The depression brought cuts of about 20%, and it was not until 1942 that the levels were returned to those of 1929. These salaries were in line with those of similar state universities. Only a few privileged institutions did not reduce salaries during the depression: Vanderbilt continued to pay full professors between $3,500.00 and $5,000.00, and Harvard paid its professors between $8,000.00 and $12,000.00. Even allowing for the greater purchasing power of the dollar in the twenties and thirties these were not handsome salaries!

Thaler in Ports and Happy Havens gives the details of what he received as a full professor during his tenure at the University. He came in 1923 at $3,250.00 and by 1929 had received raises to $4,000.00, which, he states, was about average pay for that rank, and it must be remembered that this was "top pay" in the Department and the University. For the lower ranks it would have been about one half--perhaps one reason why so many instructors left after one or two years. In 1961 Thaler reports that his basic salary was $11,000.00 (p. 213), which would have been the top pay for a professor at the University's Knoxville campus (still below the top pay of Harvard thirty years before).

I do not have information about the changes in faculty salaries since those times, but salaries today in both dollar terms and in purchasing power are greatly improved from the good (or not so good) old days. In addition to low salaries there were no fringe benefits, and not until the mid-fifties did the University provide a funded retirement program with TIAA and join the federal social security system.

See James R. Montgomery, <u>Threshold of a New Day</u>, pp. 171-73, for details and tables for these early years.

CHAPTER VII

CONTINUATION AND CHANGE; INCREASING NUMBERS; THE KNICKERBOCKER, STEWART AND FISHER YEARS: 1962-1978

The retirement of Hodges in 1962 brought an end to an era that had begun in the 1920s and early 1930s. It is difficult to overestimate the importance of the good foundation which Hodges (together with Thaler, Parker, and Emperor) laid for the subsequent growth and distinction of English studies. The last chapter noted the retirement in 1958 of Dean Hesler after twenty-four years as dean of liberal arts and the coming of a new dean, English Professor Kenneth L. Knickerbocker. Dr. Andrew D. Holt succeeded to the presidency of the University in 1958, and soon thereafter employed as academic vice-president, Dr. Herman Spivey, dean of the graduate school at the University of Kentucky and a former professor of English at Kentucky and the University of Florida. As I considered a topic or title for this chapter I thought of calling the Holt-Spivey years the golden years because this was a period when the University and its several departments were truly "Reaching for Greatness." Spivey introduced this phrase into his speeches and sought to popularize the phrase and all that it stood for. We hear an echo or variant of this phrase today in the establishment of Chairs of Excellence, a program promoted by Governor Alexander.

Before Hodges retired, Knickerbocker had expressed a wish to resign from the deanship and to return to the Department, and since the headship was shortly to be vacant, it was agreeable to the administration and the professors of English (who, by the way, were consulted) for Knickerbocker to take over. I do not think that Dean Knickerbocker after he assumed the office of dean in 1958 favored the English Department over other departments, but I know that promotions and additions to the staff came more readily than they had during the long, dry spell of Hesler's last years. A new president, a new academic vice-president, and a new college dean certainly played a role in this new spirit of liberality. Dr. Alvin Nielsen, professor of physics and head of that department, succeeded Knickerbocker as dean in 1962 and served until 1977, when Dr. Robert G. Landen, an historian, succeeded Nielsen.

The popular and universally-liked President Holt with invaluable advice and support from Vice-President Spivey, turned the University, already large in numbers and increasing in resources, into a distinguished university with first-class programs in teaching, research, and public service. I think that Holt joins President Dabney and President Ayres in making a trio of the most able presidents ever to preside over the destiny of the University of Tennessee.

Although a history of English studies is not the place to record the many changes in the organization and expansion of the University, some mention of changes is necessary. First, the tremendous increase in enrollments after the low points of the early 1950s brought pressures on every segment of the institution. Fortunately, President Holt was successful in securing funding from the legislature and in inducing private donors to fund special programs. A building program moved the center of the University westward from the Hill. The English Department moved in 1967 into spacious quarters in the McClung Tower. University enrollments grew rapidly and reached a peak of about thirty thousand, but today the number has declined to a more manageable figure of twenty-five thousand on the Knoxville campus. The University drastically changed its organization from an institution largely confined to the Knoxville campus to a statewide system in which the president became the president of all the campuses in the state with each campus headed by a chancellor. There are some who still long nostalgically for a bygone and simpler day when a less structured organization sufficed, but the new way affords much more support for exciting new programs in all fields. In the simpler days adequate funding for almost any program was almost non-existent, and I think no one wished to return to those not-so-good old days.

The increases in staff and enrollments which had begun in the 1940s and increased in the 1960s made new courses and new areas of study within the field of English studies not only desirable but imperative. The coming of Professors Davis, DeWolfe Miller, and Nathalia Wright in the late 1940s provided American literature with a strong trio of advocates. These three able professors ensured that

American literature would become one of the strengths of the Department. Davis's specialty was colonial American literature and history; hence several courses at both undergraduate and graduate level were introduced soon after his arrival in 1948. The consequence was that many master's theses and doctoral dissertations came to be written in that field because of his interest. The one-quarter course in Southern Literature became a two-quarter course, and single-quarter courses in Melville, Hawthorne, Whitman, Emily Dickinson, Henry James, and Howells found their way into the curriculum either with single-author emphasis or in various combinations to accommodate the interests and specialties of this trio.

In the 1960s many new, younger members of the Department pushed for new courses and alternative ways of doing things that had seemed to many senior staff quite comfortable and satisfactory. In the late 1960s the Department inaugurated a series of reading courses for graduate students to complement the traditional chronologically arranged and more specialized seminars. Some of these reading courses were designed to help doctoral students fill in gaps in their preparation for the much dreaded comprehensives for the Ph.D. and to help M.A. students to read in new areas. The course expressly prohibited term papers, the reading assignments were extensive (some students thought unreasonably so!), and the progress of the students was monitored by largely factual tests. An "Introduction to Literary Research" was introduced in 1968 and was particularly helpful for beginning graduate students, many of whom were unfamiliar with the resources of a large research library. G. T. Wright inaugurated the course. When he left for Minnesota, I then took over, and, on my retirement, John Fisher became the professor in charge, introducing the students to the uses of computers in scholarly research. Former students have testified to its helpfulness, and the conclusion must be that this bit of innovation was successful.

Other courses and areas were also introduced. The increasing importance of Black Literature led to the beginning of that program in the 1960s with a one-quarter upper-division course, but by 1971 it became a sophomore-level course that could be substituted for one quarter of

the sophomore literature survey. Samuel McMillan started
this program, in which Gloria Johnson and Donna Walter (who
later completed a doctoral dissertation on Doris Lessing in
1977), assisted him. McMillan in 1975-76 received a
Danforth Fellowship to enable him to further his studies in
this field at Yale University. Upon his resignation in
1976, the Department in 1977 moved to expand its offerings
in Black Literature--to enable it to become a vital part of
the University's commitment to a program of Black Studies--
by securing the services of R. Baxter Miller, a Brown Ph.D.,
who came to the Department from Haverford College as an
associate professor to implement the program. Since his
coming new courses both at the undergraduate and graduate
level have been introduced, and three doctoral dissertations
in that field have been completed. John Shields wrote a
dissertation on Phyllis Wheatley, William Barnett on the
novelist Richard Wright, and Emmanuel Nelson on the
novelists James Baldwin and John Rechy. The catalogs of
these years reveal such additional entries as a two-quarter
course in English culture, a senior survey of British
Literature, Women Writers in English and American
Literature, Literature and Film, Advanced Fiction Writing,
and the Writing of Poetry--all in place by the mid-
seventies.

Twentieth-century literature was another notable area
of expansion, partly induced by the popularity of the
courses already offered, especially the year-long course in
modern drama taught for many years by Thaler and Soper.
Soper, by the way, continued to teach the course after he
became the head of the new Department of Speech and Theatre.
The contemporary novel of the western world (Proust, Joyce,
Mann, and others) was a natural extension of the three-
quarter sequence in comparative literature. Similarly, the
three-quarter course in the English novel was expanded to a
fourth quarter to include Forster and more recent British
novelists. The course in the American novel was likewise
expanded to include Faulkner and Hemingway. Similar
expansion followed for British and American poetry. The
provision of courses in special topics has provided the
experimental instructor with the opportunity to teach and
organize an occasional course around a modern author in
which he has a special interest. Twentieth-century

literature received a final recognition when a year-long seminar at the graduate level came into being. The twentieth century was, after all, well along by the mid-sixties!

Earlier chapters of this departmental history have described or mentioned the student interest in the writing of poetry, fiction, and essays from the publication of the University of Tennessee Magazine in 1842-43, and similar magazines in the 1890s and 1920s. These were informally done and had received voluntary extra-curricular support from University faculty. By the 1940s, however, the Department had introduced a course in the writing of fiction taught by Baudin, Lee, Daniel and Mooney (among others). In 1965 the Department employed Robert Y. Drake, Jr., to fill the post of Stephen Mooney, who had resigned to go to the University of Tennessee, Martin. Drake has continued to teach the course at least once a year. A second course labeled Advanced Fiction Writing was introduced later together with a course in the Writing of Poetry, taught by Richard Kelly. An old course, Expository Writing (or Advanced Composition) had been in the curriculum since the late 1920s and was taught by Roscoe Parker, whose textbook (Advanced Composition with Harry Robbins) published by Prentice-Hall in 1933 provided (and can still provide) thorough and wise guidance for any one venturing into that field. I do not know how "creative" such a course may be, but the Department offered it with some regularity to a small group of interested students. Dr. Kate Adams praised the Parker textbook very highly when I asked for information to help in the writing of this departmental history.

When John Fisher became head of the Department in 1976 he wished to introduce several new programs and to strengthen some already in existence, and among these was the small program in creative writing. For that purpose he recruited Jon Manchip White, a graduate of St. Catherine's College, Cambridge, who had been successfully teaching and heading a program in creative writing at the University of Texas, El Paso. White, a writer versatile in fiction, poetry, biography, history, and travel, had a formidable list of two dozen books to his credit. To the courses already in the program White added such other courses as Advanced Poetry Writing, Writing Drama, Writing the

Screenplay and Television Play, Writing Science Fiction and
Fantasy, Writing the Detective and Mystery Story. The
creative writing staff was appropriately increased in 1980
with Marilyn Kallet, a published poet and a Ph.D. from
Rutgers, whose responsibility was the teaching of the
courses in poetry. Arthur Smith came in 1986 and, like
Marilyn Kallet, was already embarked upon a notable literary
career.

From a program with a few scattered courses for
undergraduates the program now comprises courses up to the
graduate level offering a student who is interested in
creative writing a systematic step-by-step advance from one
stage to the next. Graduate courses include (1987) the
writing of children's literature and experimental and avant-
garde fiction. In addition to the undergraduate enrollment
the program has been popular with entering graduate
students. About one third choose a master's program with an
emphasis upon writing, which might include technical writing
and editing.

In the 1970s the Department moved to increase its
offerings in language, linguistics, and dialectology.
Courses in the history of the language, modern English
grammar, and a graduate course in the English language were
already offered. In fact, a hundred years ago the Professor
of English often had the title of Professor of Language and
Literature, and the study of English often emphasized the
philological at the expense of the literary. A play by
Shakespeare might be studied for its linguistic examples
rather than for its purely aesthetic virtues. The new
program began in the winter and spring quarters of 1970,
1972, and 1975 when the Department had as a visiting
professor, Dr. Harold Orton, professor emeritus of Leeds
University (England), who offered a course in dialect.
Orton also taught the courses in Old and Middle English.
Orton's monumental <u>Survey of English Dialects</u> was just
coming to a conclusion. During his brief tenure in the
University he directed two dissertations in American
dialect, specifically as spoken in East Tennessee, and he
was the chief speaker at a conference in dialectology in
April 1970 in honor of the 175th anniversary of the
University, supported by the Better English Fund. The
papers, edited by Lorraine Burghardt were published as

Dialectology: Problems and Perspectives. Nathalia Wright
assisted Orton in his Word Geography of England and also
published a Questionnaire for the Investigation of American
Regional English: Based on the Work Sheets of The
Linguistic Atlas of the United States and Canada.

In 1975 Dr. Bethany K. Dumas, a specialist in
linguistics and dialectology, came to the Department as an
Associate Professor to continue the work that had been
started. Her work, however, was not a direct continuation
of Orton's work, although she has continued her interests in
dialectology, and has directed dissertations on the folk
speech of the Cumberland Plateau (Guy H. Bailey, III, in
1979), "Variation in Appalachian English" (James R. Reese in
1977), and "A Dictionary of American Slang on Historical
Principles: The Letter A" (Jonathan E. Lighter). Since her
arrival Dumas has taught several courses such as Appalachian
English, Women's Language, Stylistics, Computational
Stylistics--to mention a few examples. In addition to a
course on Language in the Judicial Process Dumas has
chaired a number of programs including the two-year-old
Speaker Series on Law and Linguistics, jointly sponsored by
the College of Law and the Program in Linguistics.

The importance of the program in language was
emphasized when in 1977 the Department decided to vary its
degree offerings by allowing students to choose from one of
the three concentrations: literature, English language, or
writing.

English as a Second Language had, like most of the
programs developed by the Department, a modest beginning in
the 1940s. C. P. Lee taught a special section of Freshman
English restricted to foreign students with the hope that
with some special attention these students could, after one
or two quarters, take their place in the regular sections of
Freshman English. In 1964 Professor Ralph Walker came to
direct a new program to care for the diverse and special
needs of several hundred students who came from all over the
world with the largest numbers from the Middle East, Latin
America, and Asia. Approximately 200-300 students come
through the program each year, and some 4,500 students from
the ESL program have taken the English Placement Exam.

In recent years the staff of English as a Second

Language has expanded to include instruction to help prepare
upper-division undergraduates and graduate students to teach
in this new and expanding field. In these courses students
become acquainted with the structure of American English,
current theories of second language acquisition, and various
methodologies and techniques for teaching English as a
second language. They are given the opportunity to observe
the classes on campus within the English Department and at
the English Language Institute, to work with the teachers of
these classes, and eventually to conduct classes of their
own under the supervision of the staff of English as a
Second Language. Many of these students have subsequently
gone abroad to teach in Europe, Asia, the Middle East, and
Latin America.

The staff of English as a Second Language numbers
(1987) between four and six, with two of these positions
being faculty positions. Dr. Ilona Leki, who had been
working in the program, succeeded Walker as the director
upon his retirement.

Two programs with which the Department was closely
identified for many years were dropped: the Junior English
Exam and the Statewide English Program. The University,
through the University Committee or Student English, dropped
the requirement --in place since the 1920s--of the Junior
English Exam. This exam had been an added burden for
members of the staff, who were required to grade the test
papers three or four times a year, and the English Writing
Laboratory was largely populated by the more or less unhappy
juniors (even seniors) who had failed to pass this by-no-
means rigorous test of basic writing ability. The dropping
of the Statewide English Program, a favorite project of Dr.
Hodges, coincided with the retirement of Professor Charles
Webb in 1970, who had represented the Department for many
years in this program.

Up to this point my narrative has emphasized growth in
courses, introduction of new areas of study, increases in
enrollments and additions to staff. But this trend did not
continue. By the early 1970s the general national movement
away from the humanities and in favor of a wide variety of
socially oriented subjects gained momentum. A committee in
the College of Liberal Arts, attuned to these trends, sought
a major revision in the requirements for degrees offered by

the College. In this struggle--a bitter and protracted one fought in many faculty meetings--the English Department, to put it quite simply, lost out. The degree requirements as they involved Freshman and Sophomore English were drastically lowered, and since most of the enrollments and need for staff involved those courses, the damage was severe. The sophomore survey of English and American literature, long a requirement for any degree in the College, became only an option among many courses. Although students who elected to seek a degree in liberal arts might be presumed to have a certain predilection towards literature, I discovered that in my sections of sophomore literature only two or three students were from liberal arts and the others came from the colleges of business, home economics, and engineering, which still retained a literature requirement.

The committee made further changes by altering the credit hours earned in courses at the elementary level. Courses that met three hours a week had traditionally carried three quarter hours of credit, but the new arrangement called for four hours credit for these courses. The result was that the year-long three-quarter course in Freshman English now became a two-quarter course. This new two-quarter course with eight hours of credit now satisfied the Freshman English requirement. In this matter the English Department was not consulted since we were assured that we would teach as much in two quarters as we had in three quarters--so great was the faith of the committee in the skills of those teaching in the Department! Since Freshman English was a requirement in other colleges, those colleges also reduced their English requirements. The new credit-hour arrangement also affected the sophomore courses.

The English Department did its best to justify the additional hour of credit in freshman and sophomore courses, and it succeeded after a year or two in restoring the three-quarter, nine-hour requirement in Freshman English. Furthermore, the Department did not dilute its three-hour upper-division courses by changing them to four-credit hour courses meeting three hours a week. For many students throughout the College, however, the new arrangement was a great bargain as they did no more work for four hours of credit than they had for three. Since the English

Department continued to offer only three hours of credit for advanced courses meeting three hours a week, it lost elective enrollment to other departments that chose to offer four hours credit for three meetings. For some faculty the new arrangement meant a reduced teaching load, as each instructor was producing more credit hours although not having to meet so many classes for so many hours.

The revision of the curriculum and the requirements for the degree led to a broadening of courses at the sophomore level as the Department sought to respond to the interests of the students. Quarter courses labeled as introductions to drama, poetry, and the novel were offered as alternatives to the traditional chronological surveys. A further experimental course, Special Topics, permitted the teacher of the course to devise a course around a particular theme: examples of two that were offered, we are told with success, were on Arthurian literature and the Byronic hero. These new offerings attracted a following either because of the attractiveness of the subject matter or of the instructor teaching the course. For sophomore students contemplating a major in English a Colloquium for English majors was provided as a preparatory review of the major. Curricula and requirements for degrees are never static, and the change by the University from the quarter to the semester system has now resulted in a complete restructuring of courses and requirements. These new arrangements will be effective in the academic year 1988-89.

The expanded graduate program inaugurated in 1945 had by 1970 reached its quarter century, and had achieved an enrollment in the range of 150 students. A special study of the graduate program in 1975 mentioned that the Department had graduated 123 Ph.D.s and over 500 M.A.s and M.A.C.T.s. During the first twenty to twenty-five years the Department had been able to place its graduates advantageously, but by the early seventies the supply of Ph.D.s and M.A.s in English and in many related fields was outrunning the demand. As a result of the lower market for the Department's graduates a small decline in graduate enrollment took place. The Department also sought to add new areas of study and to give more options to those seeking advanced degrees. The coming of new persons into the Department assisted in this gradual change--especially the arrival of Professor Fisher in 1972.

The departmental requirements for the Ph.D. were traditional. The student was expected to be prepared in a wide range of areas in English and American literature and to present proficiency in two languages, usually French, German, or Latin. The Department has always discouraged students from receiving three degrees from the University (B.A., M.A., and Ph.D.), but a few exceptions were made. As soon as the doctoral program was begun, the decision was made not to hire as permanent members of the staff its own Ph.D.s, and this policy has been enforced without exception, even though pressures have been exerted for an exception or two. Thus the Department has spared itself the problems of inbreeding.

By 1962 the graduate program was prospering so that a more elaborate system of supervision was needed. The director of graduate studies (Davis) was now assisted by two associate directors (Nathalia Wright and Curry) with a separate office, secretary and telephone. These three professors shared in the direction and responsibility, often tedious, for answering the considerable volume of correspondence, preparing a brochure, recommending applicants for graduate and teaching assistantships, arranging for the examinations for masters and doctoral students, and doing whatever was necessary for the smooth running of the program including conferring with individual graduate students about their program of study. Responsibility for the summer quarter rotated among these three. The graduate committee in the Department--which some regarded for a time as the most influential in the Department--consisted of the director, the two associate directors, the head of the Department, and the director of Freshman English. One by-product of the increased graduate enrollment was that the Department supplied the University with a large pool of teaching assistants who gradually undertook much of the teaching of freshman and some sophomore English classes--at a low cost to the institution.

In 1973 the directorship of the graduate program came to Percy Adams, who ably continued the program until 1980. Richard Kelly succeeded him. The present director is Nancy Goslee, and her associate, Charles Maland.

In 1966 the University and the English Department instituted a new degree: Master of Arts in College Teaching designed for students who wished to teach in community, junior, and smaller four-year colleges. The program was a two-year one, required proficiency in one foreign language, and gave the student the opportunity to gain experience in college teaching. The idea was a good one, but the reduced demand for college teachers made the program redundant, and it was later abandoned. The Ph.D. was still the sine qua non for a career in college or university teaching.

The increased enrollments of these years led to appointments of new assistant and associate professors. Not since the post-war expansion of the forties (1945-49) were so many new appointments made. Knickerbocker's first appointments (1963-64) were Francelia Butler (Virginia) and Neil Isaacs (Brown). Dr. Butler, who has become a well-known specialist in children's literature, left after two years for the University of Connecticut. Isaacs, a medievalist, went in 1971 to the University of Maryland. 1964-65 marked the appointment of Samuel H. McMillan (Texas), who resigned in 1976; Edward Bratton (Illinois); and Ralph Walker (M.A., Texas), who was to supervise the teaching of English as a second language, and retired in 1987. 1965-66 witnessed the largest number of appointments ever made in any one year: Robert Y. Drake, Jr. (Yale) as an associate professor, and as assistant professors: Allison Ensor (Indiana), James Gill (North Carolina), Richard M. Kelly (Duke), Bobby J. Leggett (Florida), and Richard Penner (Colorado). Twenty-one instructors were also appointed. Promotions also were abundant: Associate Professors Hansen, Sanders, and Stockton were made full professors, and Assistant Professor Isaacs an associate. 1965-66 certainly was a record year for good things happening to many people. In 1968-69 Lorraine Burghardt (Chicago) was appointed an assistant professor, and H. Willard Reninger, Knickerbocker's collaborator in Interpreting Literature, was appointed as a visiting professor for the following year. In 1969-70, D. Allen Carroll (North Carolina) and Frank K. Robinson (Texas) were appointed as assistant professors, followed in 1970-71 by Barry Gaines (Wisconsin), David Goslee (Yale), and Nancy Goslee (Yale). Dr. Percy Adams returned as a full professor after four years at Louisiana State University. Mary Richards (Wisconsin), a medievalist, was the only one of four assistant professors appointed in 1971-72 who remained. The others, who stayed briefly, were: Richard T. Goode, David C. Kwinn, and Paul Merchant. 1972 was another good one for promotions: Wheeler to full professor, McMillan to associate, and Carroll and Robinson to tenured assistant professors.

Since the roster is chronologically arranged and records the yearly addition of new staff, I am not mentioning in the narrative every arrival and departure. A few appointments at the full-professor level, however, should be mentioned: John H. Fisher (1972), the first John C. Hodges Professor of English, a medievalist and Chaucer specialist, who had served as Executive Secretary of the Modern Language Association and was later its president; William H. Shurr (1981) in American literature and author of books on Dickinson and Melville; Daniel J. Schneider (1978) in modern British literature, who had published books on D. H. Lawrence and Henry James; and Jon Manchip White (1977), author of twenty books of fiction, poetry, travel, and archaeology, came to the Department to head and expand the creative writing program.

Although professors of all ranks taught freshman and sophomore classes as part of their regular program, the Department also employed a corps of permanent, often part-time, instructors, to teach the basic courses, and this group came to be the group on which the Department depended for reliable instruction year after year. These were all M.A.s (a few had Ph.D.s) with experience. Several have served with distinction for long periods, some as long as twenty years. I may forget a few names, but I wish to mention particularly these instructors (some have retired, and Sanders and Martin have died): Polly Adams, Eleanor Badgett, Esther Bare, Dr. Delle Craven, Wynn J. Curtis, Kathleen Feerick, Eddie Francisco, Louise Fuller, Clyde Hoffman, Katherine Moore, David Powell, Eleanora Overbey, Howard Sanders, Margaret Simpson, Penelope Tschantz, Jeanne Schneider, and Dr. Mineko Lewis. Two instructors from the group, in recognition of their excellent work, plus their publication or special service, were made assistant professors: Patsy Hammontree and Carolyn Martin. If it had

not been for this group of hard-working, dedicated teachers
the Department could not have offered the students and the
University the high quality of instruction at the elementary
level which it has provided over the years. Many of these
experienced instructors also served as mentors to beginning
teaching assistants and instructors. I think this group
deserves all the recognition and praise which the
Department can give for their long years of service.

I think it unnecessary in an account of the Department
to speak in detail of the student unrest on the campus
during the late sixties and early seventies as Greene's
history of the University gives a full account of the
events. The University was spared the extensive violence
that tragically marred the tranquillity of many campuses.
Since most of my own work involved the graduate students
and upper-division classes, I led a relatively sheltered
life during those years. I noticed, however, in teaching
sophomore-level and some upper-division courses not only
apathy and indifference--always present to a certain extent-
-but also a marked hostility among some students to the
formal requirements of classes and demands for regular
attendance and careful preparation of assignments and papers
on a timely basis. As a consequence, the drop-out rate was
abnormally high. A few faculty in some departments were
prominent in expressions of protest and unrest, but the
English Department was not involved in the occasional campus
demonstrations. My own judgment is that the few years of
unrest had no lasting influence on the Department or its
future. My only regret is that many students in those years
missed valuable educational opportunities and short-changed
themselves.

The Hodges Better English Fund

John C. Hodges, the former head of the Department, died
on July 7, 1967. Prior to his death he had established the
Better English Fund, which at the time of his death had
assets of $200,000.00. His will placed the income from the
fund at the discretion of the full professors (and the
professors emeriti) of the Department for the purposes
implied by the title. His will further provided that the

Better English Fund would receive the annual royalties from the very successful Harbrace College Handbook. As a result of this most generous bequest the fund has now (1987) reached approximately two million dollars. The Department cannot spend the principal, but the annual increments have resulted in a steadily rising annual income from the Fund. See Annual Report, 1967-68.

The story of the fund's inception, as I remember it, was that after the publication of the Handbook in 1941 and its adoption by the Department as a textbook for Freshman English, Hodges set aside the royalties which would accrue to him from the sale of the Handbook on the UT campus. Later he added to the Fund the royalties that would come from the sale of the Handbook at other colleges in the state. He also made additional contributions to the Fund during his lifetime.

As the head of the Department he had been acutely aware of the inadequacy of institutional funds for providing desirable and often necessary support for faculty development, aid for the research projects of individuals, financial assistance for travel to professional conventions, and scholarships for English undergraduate majors and graduate students. Since he had certainly been frustrated by going through channels of administrative approval for every expenditure, he prudently provided that the professors in the Department, whose good judgment he quite obviously respected, were to be the judges of how the funds would be spent. He wished the emeritus professors to be involved because they would provide continuity, and for a few decades they would be reliable interpreters of his wishes--and hopes--for the Department and its objectives.

Each year a small budget committee of the professors prepares a budget which is then submitted for approval to the group at an annual meeting. Special requests, if they cannot wait, may be approved or rejected at special meetings called during the year.

The expenditures from the Fund have been so numerous that they cannot all be listed, but a few of the first ones can be mentioned here: scholarships for undergraduate majors, scholarships or non-service fellowships for graduate students, annual grants to the Library for the purchase of special items, supplements to the meager travel allowances supplied by the University, fees for visiting lecturers finally culminating in the series of Hodges Lectures by nationally known scholars and with subsidized publication by the University of Tennessee Press, subsidies for several books published by present faculty and former students, and, finally, funding for the first John C. Hodges Professorship of English in 1972.

At the present time a generous portion of the funds is awarded to students: six undergraduate scholarships and several graduate scholarships and fellowships. Each year Hodges Teaching Awards in the form of a modest cash gift are given to teachers in the freshman program (both to beginners and veterans) as recognition for good work in teaching. A few years ago the Fund began to provide the faculty with mini-sabbaticals for portions of a year and are designed to provide an important benefit which the University does not provide. The Department sponsors Tennessee Studies in Literature and Restoration: Studies in English Literary Culture for which the Hodges Fund provides a subsidy to assist publication and to provide clerical help and office space. The Chaucer Society now has its headquarters in the Department, and a small grant has been awarded this society to aid it publications.

Since the Library (the new Library is now named the John C. Hodges Library) was always a special concern of Hodges, the Fund regularly makes a gift to the Library and assists on occasion with the purchase of special items. Several large endowment funds in the Library--notably that in memory of Richard Beale Davis--were either established or augmented by gifts from the Fund.

Library Endowment Funds With An English Connection

James Douglas Bruce Fund	$5,005.00
Mamie C. Johnston Fund	5,451.77
Durant Da Ponte Fund	3,899.43
Thomas L. James Fund (a Hodges kinsman)	4,531.42
Kenneth Curry Fund	3,778.17
John C. Hodges--UTK Alumni Library	

Endowment Fund	98,583.15
John C. Hodges Books for English Library	
Endowment Fund	39,574.02
Richard B. Davis Humanities Endowment Fund	112,359.98

$273,181.83

Except for the Bruce Fund (1923) all these funds are due either to solicitations by Dr. Hodges, personal gifts he made to these funds, or gifts made by the Department of English from the Hodges Better English Fund. These figures are from the U. T. Treasurer's annual report for 1986.

When John Fisher assumed the headship of the Department in 1976 he sought new ways of doing old things. I think it is fair to say that in most ways the headships of Knickerbocker and Stewart continued (with gradual growth and necessary modifications) the pattern that had been established during the Hodges years. Fisher persuaded with some difficulty the administration to give the Department additional secretarial assistance and to create a new administrative office by throwing together two small inside offices. The Department by this time had 150 teaching faculty (including graduate assistants), more than 300 sections, more than 6,000 students, and had simply outgrown its old, cramped quarters.

Fisher's second change was more sweeping as he put into place a new organization of the Department. He instituted an Administrative Committee to make departmental decisions: the Head, the Associate Head (a new position), the Director of Graduate Studies, the Director of Undergraduate Studies, the Director of Freshman Composition. These five were augmented by two elected members: one full professor and one from the ranks of assistant and associate professor. A later modification in the bylaws provided that no more than one of the two was to be a full professor, and allowing for both elected members to be from the assistant and associate ranks. This arrangement diluted the decision-making responsibilities of the former graduate committee and the group of full professors who had traditionally advised the Head. It also provided a group which was both representative of the faculty and involved in the day-to-day operations of the Department which could both advise the head on departmental administration and provide coordination of recommendations on curriculum and personnel for decisions by the faculty as a whole.

The expanded program in creative writing, already described, was soon in place, and students were able to major in English language and writing as well as the traditional literature major. Fisher also made a beginning in the field of technical writing, later expanded. The tremendous influx of foreign students without competence in English was taxing the Department's program in English as a foreign language. Fisher persuaded the administration to create an English Institute for foreign students under the auspices of Continuing Education. Dr. Dale Myers, an associate professor and a linguist in the Department, left the Department to become the head of this Institute.

Fisher also inaugurated the Hodges Lectures. Unfortunately, these lectures, although presented by scholar-professors of national and international renown, never attracted the audiences hoped for and did not achieve the eminence of several well-known series at other universities upon which they were modeled. The series has been discontinued, but can well be revived when deemed desirable. The lectures with their accompanying publication by the University of Tennessee Press constitute a record of a noble effort of the Department.

A more successful program has been the frequent readings by young poets and novelists brought to the campus by the creative writing program. These readings have attracted a regular, if somewhat special, audience.

A graduate student, who had entered in the pre-Fisher years and then returned in the post-Fisher era, characterized Fisher as "probably the single greatest catalyst for change in the UT English department" and noted the changes in the Department from those of the early seventies:

When I returned in 1982, there was a highly developed

TA-training program, professors were writing about Andy Griffith and Elvis Presley, the bibliography class was using computers, there were courses in tech writing and editing, groups of faculty and students were meeting in teachers' homes to discuss deconstruction, and graduate students were permitted to write dissertations on such non-traditional subjects as lawyers' abuses of rhetoric.

Although the Fisher tenure was for only two years, his headship did much to stimulate the thinking of the Department into new directions and to influence a reluctant administration into doing things for a Department that (I think) was for far too long just taken for granted.

After the retirement of Hodges, Knickerbocker became head of the department until he left in 1971 to become University Vice-President for Academic Affairs. Bain T. Stewart succeeded him and served as head for five years until 1976 when John H. Fisher took over for two years until 1978. Joseph B. Trahern, Jr., a Princeton Ph.D., an associate professor of English at the University of Illinois, Champaign, and a native Tennessean, succeeded Fisher. Trahern was the first department head, incidentally, to come directly from outside the university since 1900 when James Douglas Bruce came to be head. As I have said elsewhere, my impression was that Knickerbocker and Stewart continued the pattern of organization and basic orientation of the English Department which Hodges left as his legacy. Of course, the growth in staff and enrollments meant that changes and expansion took place, as this chapter has chronicled. Professors were left very much to do their teaching and research in their own way, and since the Department had a group of able persons with excellent training and high professional standards, the rather easy atmosphere of collegiality worked very well insofar as I experienced and observed all that was going on. The Department during all those years was and has continued to be essentially harmonious and has never experienced the harsh divisiveness and schisms that have marred some departments. Most members of the Department manage to be on at least speaking terms with each other! This congenial spirit has been fostered by the five heads from Hodges to Trahern and has been an important factor in the good reputation for teaching and research which the Department has enjoyed.

I announced my intention not to make special mention of those who joined the Department after 1945, but I am making an exception for Professor Richard Beale Davis, who, I think, was one of the most distinguished professors in the University, and certainly should be celebrated along with Bruce, Thaler, and Hodges as among our "shining lights." His scholarly writing and his pioneer research into the field of colonial American Southern literature was extensive and thorough, and his three-volume study, Intellectual Life in the Colonial South, 1585-1763, is one of the outstanding monuments of American literary scholarship. The Association of American Publishers awarded him its National Book Award in History at a ceremony on April 25, 1979 at Carnegie Hall. The University recognized the importance of this achievement when Chancellor Reese presented President Reagan, on a visit to the campus, with a copy of this book as a memento of his trip to Knoxville.

I have been told that some students found him rather formidable, but I know of no one in the Department who was more genuinely interested in the welfare of his students and in their post-University careers. He had high standards for his students as well as for himself, and many will attest to the fact that they excelled because he held them to a peak of achievement and made them discover, when pushed, that they could exceed the modest limits which they had imposed upon themselves. The esteem and affection which his former students had for him can be seen in the sixteen essays which they contributed to a memorial volume, No Fairer Land: Studies in Southern Literature Before 1900, edited by J. Lasley Dameron and James W. Mathews (1986).

Visiting Professors

The Department has enjoyed the presence of visiting professors from time to time, and these have proved stimulating to both students and faculty. A few of these visitors are listed below.

1925-26   *Herman S. Ficke.*

1946+   *Dean Edwin R. Hunter of Maryville College taught several summers in the late 1940s, and graduate students found him a worthwhile and genial taskmaster.*

1950   *Nevill Coghill, medievalist and well-known modernizer of Chaucer, of Oxford University, was on campus during the summer of 1950. Coghill had been the tutor of C.P. Lee, former Rhodes Scholar and member of the Department.*

1962-63   *Boyd A. Litzinger, a UT Ph.D., professor at St. Bonaventure College, taught Victorian courses with the rank of Visiting Associate Professor.*

1968-69   *H. Willard Reninger, University of Northern Iowa, andco-author with Knickerbocker of Interpreting Literature, spent 1968-69 on campus and proved to be a stimulating teacher.*

1970+   *Harold Orton, University of Leeds, taught the winter and spring terms of 1970, 1972, 1973, including a course in dialect studies.*

1975-78   *Herman E. Spivey, former academic vice-president of the University and professor of English, Universities of Florida and*

Kentucky, served three years as a professor following his retirement from his earlier positions. An able teacher and scholar in American literature, he contributed greatly to the Department's program.

1976-77   James L. Allen, Professor of English, University of Hawaii, Hilo, whose specialty has been Yeats and the Irish Renaissance, was exchanging posts with Professor DeWolfe Miller, who spent the year at the Univesity of Hawaii. Allen had been an instructor in the Department during 1954-46.

1977+   Wilma Dykeman Stokely, the well-known Tennessee writer, has taught a class in writing almost regularly every spring term and was recently made an adjunct professor of English. Mrs. Stokely has long been a strong supporter of the University, the College of Liberal Arts (of which she is a "visitor"), and a valued friend of the English Department.

1978   Charles Shattuck, University of Illinois, Champaign, taught during the fall quarter.

1986-87   Daniel J. Cahill, the University of Northern Iowa, taught courses in twentieth-century British and American literature as a National Faculty Exchange Professor.

1987   R. Baird Shuman, University of Illinois, taught during the winter and spring quarters.

1988   *Robert L. Taylor, Bucknell University, taught*
                during the academic year as a National
                Faculty Exchange Professor.

The Department and Learned Societies

The Department has always been well represented at the meetings of the South Atlantic Modern Language Association, and in recent years has entertained its former students and staff at a reception during this annual meeting. Two professors of English have served as presidents: Richard Beale Davis and Nathalia Wright. For several years Professor Edward Bratton served as Executive Secretary, and the University and the Department provided office and secretarial assistance to the Association. Dr. W. Donald Kay, one of our Ph.D.s, then Professor of English at the University of Alabama, succeeded Bratton as Executive Director and Editor of the South Atlantic Review *when the Association's office was moved to Alabama.*

Two professors in the Department have also served as presidents of the Modern Language Association of America: James Douglas Bruce in 1918 and John H. Fisher in 1974. Prior to his coming to the University, Fisher had served as Executive Director of the Association and as editor of PMLA *from 1963 to 1971. In addition, members of the Department have regularly attended these national meetings, held committee posts, and appeared on the programs.*

I am sure that there are other learned societies in which members of the professorial staff have held top offices. Fisher has been elected (1987) to the presidency of the Medieval Academy and has served as president of the new Chaucer Society.

State Associations

The Department's association with the Tennessee Philological Association and Tennessee College English Association has been a long one. In 1911 the University and the Department hosted the fifth annual meeting of the Tennessee Philological Association and afterwards the meetings of 1915, 1921, 1928, 1935, 1946, and 1983. Several members of the Department served as presidents of the Association: Alwin Thaler (1956), John C. Hodges (1958), and Allison Ensor (1978). Many UTK alumni have served as president, including Eleanor Mitchell (1987), Charlotte Beck (1986), Charles Hobbs (1984), Harry Merrill (1983), Lasley Dameron (1980), John Warren (1972), and Elizabeth Phillips (1966). Both professors and graduate students have read many papers at the annual meeting.

The Department has also lent its support to a newer state-wide organization: the Tennessee College English Association. In 1979 the University and the Department hosted the annual meeting, and Bain Stewart served as president in 1979-80. Several UTK alumni have served as presidents of this organization including Eleanor Mitchell, John Warren, and James Thomas. Allison Ensor has served as secretary-treasurer of the group since 1975.

CHAPTER VIII

1978-1988:   AN OVERVIEW
by
Joseph B. Trahern, Jr. and Edward W. Bratton

Since Kenneth Curry retired at the end of 1978, he was understandably reluctant to attempt to record the activities of the department during the past ten years. We, by contrast, have been so fully involved in those activities from day to day that we despair of obtaining the sort of perspective on them which Curry's chapters achieve. We think, moreover, that we are too close, both in time and involvement, to the period we are reporting on to make judgments upon it. We wish to leave those to the next departmental historian and offer here a narrative of what seem to us to be the highlights of the decade, aware that the very process of selection implies some judgment but hoping that we have remembered the most important developments and have presented them in as objective a manner as we can.

FACULTY

The fall of 1978 brought four new members to the professorial staff: Trahern as Head, Daniel Schneider, who had earlier been a Visiting Professor, as Professor in 20th Century Fiction, Charles Maland in American Literature and Cinema Studies, and Marjorie Pryse in American Literature. The Department reached an agreement with Dean Landen whereby we would initiate a search for a Professor in American Literature but otherwise would seek to enlarge the professorial staff through replacements at the entry level. At Curry's retirement, the tenured and tenure-track faculty numbered thirty-two. At this writing, though a few positions remain unfilled, there are forty-four full-time faculty lines. The department managed, by this method, to obtain desperately needed additional faculty at a time that the faculty of the College of Liberal Arts was shrinking by better than twenty per cent. It was a good time to grow--the seller's market of the sixties was long gone, and the candidates available were exceptional. Marketplace factors contributed as well to a healthy stability in the faculty. Barry Gaines, who accepted a Professorship at the University of New Mexico in 1979, and Marjorie Pryse, who resigned to enter another profession, are the only tenured faculty members to have left the department during the decade until the departure of Mary Richards in the fall of 1988 to the Deanship at Auburn. We suffered, of course, from the untimely death of Carolyn Martin and from the retirements of Curry, Stewart, Adams, Wright, Walker, and Fisher, as well as from the departure to greener pastures of such promising Assistant Professors as Stephen Watt, Dorothy Denniston, and Kate Adams. But for the most part we were fortunate in being able to appoint new faculty who enlarged the departmental areas of expertise and at the same time to retain the vast majority of a faculty which was already beginning to build for the department a national reputation in research while continuing to display a longstanding commitment to quality teaching at both the graduate and undergraduate levels.

In the first wave of new Assistant Professors came Katherine Adams (Ph.D., Florida) in rhetoric and composition, Marilyn Kallet (Ph.D., Rutgers) in creative writing, Michael Keene (Ph.D., Texas) in technical writing, and Madelaine Newfield (Ph.D., Cornell) in linguistics. Newfield resigned, married, and accompanied her husband to another institution after two years; the other three provided a solid beginning to a continuing and exciting period of recruiting of younger faculty. Dr. Ilona Leki (Ph. D., Illinois) won a national search for a second full-time professorial faculty member in English as a Second Language. William Shurr (Ph.D., North Carolina) accepted the Professorship in American Literature. The second round of intensive searches for junior faculty brought us Dorothy Denniston (Ph.D., Brown) in Black Literature, George Hutchinson (Ph.D., Indiana) in American Literature, Robert Stillman (Ph.D., Pennsylvania) in Renaissance Literature, and Stephen Watt (Ph.D., Illinois) in Modern Drama. Gay Marie Logsdon, a doctoral candidate at Texas, joined us next, replacing Newfield, but left us and later completed her dissertation and took a position in technical writing. 1985 marked the arrival of Allen Dunn (Ph.D., Washington) in Criticism, Donald Samson (Ph.D., North Carolina) in Technical Writing, John Zomchick (Ph.D., Columbia) in 18th-

Century Literature. They were followed in 1986 by Linda Bensel-Meyers (Ph.D., Oregon) in Rhetoric and Composition, Jeanie Forte (Ph.D., Washington) in Modern Drama, Kathryn Riley (Ph.D., Maryland [English] and Ph.D., LSU [Linguistics]) in Linguistics, and Arthur Smith (Ph.D., Houston) in Creative Writing. Ray Wallace (D.A., Illinois State) joined us in 1987 in English as a Second Language following the retirement of Ralph Walker.

Of the twenty-three faculty in the professorial ranks appointed between 1978 and 1988, seventeen remain in the department and represent better than 40% of the current professorial staff. By sharp contrast, we have lost during the same decade only eight tenured faculty members who were here before 1978, with the result that the department has been able to enjoy the benefits of a stable faculty together with a substantial infusion of new talent.

During the tenure of Dean Robert Landen, Knoxville attorney Lindsay Young endowed a number of salary supplement chairs in the College of Liberal Arts and asked that one go to the Department of English. The first occupant of that chair was Percy Adams, and Jon Manchip White was at the same time awarded an at-large Young Professorship. At Adams's retirement, the departmental Young Professorship was awarded to Norman Sanders. Daniel Schneider was made an Alumni Distinguished Service Professor. In 1987, Dean Lorman Ratner, who succeeded Landen, established a number of Distinguished Humanities Professorships on monies raised from the National Endowment for the Humanities Challenge Grant. B. J. Leggett and William Shurr were two of the five recipients of these chairs. Three more Young Professorships were established later in the year, and one of these went to Richard Kelly. The John C. Hodges Chair of Excellence given to the Department was filled, effective August of 1988, by Professor Richard Finneran of Tulane, a distinguished Yeats scholar. Until they were discontinued in 1987 to provide more chairs for ongoing appointments, there were also a number of one-year Young Professorships, nearly one-third of which were held over a seven-year period by English faculty- -B. J. Leggett, Richard Kelly, Norman Sanders, Daniel Schneider, Robert Drake, William Shurr, R. Baxter Miller, and Jack Armistead.

A number of faculty were invited as Visiting Professors

to other institutions. Daniel Schneider became UTK's first participant in the National Faculty Exchange, spending a year at the University of Northern Colorado. Robert Drake held the Murphy Professorship at Hendrix College (1982) and conducted a seminar which brought a number of distinguished visiting writers to that campus. Marjorie Pryse visited at the University of California at Santa Cruz. Charles Maland held a Senior Lecture Fellowship at the University of Bergen, Norway (1981-82). Percy Adams was a Visiting Distinguished Professor at Texas A & M University during the fall of 1982. During 1986-87 Dorothy Denniston was the recipient of a post-doctoral fellowship at Brown University; and Ron Miller held a National Research Council Senior Fellowship at the University of North Carolina at Chapel Hill and Fisk University (and was also a UNCF Visiting Distinguished Scholar at Xavier University during part of 1987-88). Michael Lofaro and Thomas Heffernan won year-long appointments as research scholars at the National Humanities Center in Research Triangle, North Carolina. Instructor Clyde Hoffman taught for two terms in the writing program at Harvard.

DEPARTMENTAL ADMINISTRATION

In addition to the efficient administrative structure introduced by Fisher and alluded to by Curry in the preceding chapter, Trahern happily inherited most of Fisher's able staff of academic administrators. Ed Bratton continued as Associate Head, Percy Adams as Director of Graduate Studies, Mary Richards as Director of Undergraduate Studies, and David Goslee as Director of Composition. Richard Kelly replaced Norman Sanders as Associate Director of Graduate Studies. These, joined by elected representatives B. J. Leggett and Allen Carroll, made up the Administrative Committee, which functioned as the principal advising body to the Head. Office Supervisor Wanda Giles served the committee ex officio as its Secretary. Richards accepted an appointment as Assistant Dean in the Graduate School and was replaced by B. J. Leggett. In subsequent years, Don Cox replaced David Goslee, Kelly replaced Adams and was assisted first by Cox and then by Nancy Goslee, who

and was assisted first by Cox and then by Nancy Goslee, who
subsequently replaced Kelly and was assisted by Chuck
Maland, and Jack Armistead replaced Leggett. Other elected
faculty members of the committee during the period included
Kelly, Nancy Goslee, Dick Penner, Maland, Bain Stewart,
Kate Adams, Thomas Heffernan, and George Hutchinson. Leggett
and Carroll were elected for two terms. R. Baxter Miller
coordinated the program in Black Literature, Bethany Dumas
that in linguistics, Ralph Walker, succeeded by Ilona Leki,
coordinated the offerings in English as a Second Language,
and Jon Manchip White, succeeded by Marilyn Kallet, oversaw
the Creative Writing Program.

LECTURES AND SYMPOSIA

As the faculty grew in numbers and in scholarly
productivity, a substantial number of them participated
actively in professional meetings and symposia elsewhere and
several served as distinguished visiting faculty at other
research or teaching institutions. At the same time, the
decade was a busy one at home. The fall of 1978 saw the
convening on campus of a symposium on Black American
Literature and Humanism, supported by the ACLS and the
Better English Fund and organized and directed by R. Baxter
Miller. The conference brought to campus such luminaries as
poet Michael Harper, playwright Alice Childress, and
scholars George Kent, Darwin Turner, Trudier Harris, and
Richard Barksdale. Selected papers from the conference were
later published by the University Press of Kentucky. The
Hodges Lectures, described elsewhere by Curry, began that
year as well, and the new Creative Writing Program sponsored
its first conference--one which emphasized Science Fiction
and Fantasy and featured Theodore Sturgeon. The Medieval
Studies Program hosted the distinguished historian of
monasticism Jean Leclercq, Professor George Kane of Chapel
Hill, and Father Chrysogonus Waddell, composer and
musicologist, at its annual medieval festival. The following
year brought Muriel Bradbrook of Cambridge and John Russell
Brown from the National Theatre to campus in conjunction
with the Clarence Brown Company's production of As You Like
It. The distinguished theater historian Charles Shattuck

spent a term as Visiting Professor which included three
scintillating public lectures on Booth's Hamlet, famous
Shakespearean actresses, and current attitudes and trends in
productions of Shakespeare's plays. Medieval Studies brought
Larry Benson of Harvard and archaeologist Martin Biddle as
well as the Poculi Ludi Societas from the University of
Toronto. The next year brought a stellar array of modern
writers to campus as well as a quarter's visit from
Professor Cleanth Brooks. Brooks's presence prompted a visit
from his longtime friend, colleague and collaborator Robert
Penn Warren; and the two held a symposium, moderated by
Robert Drake, on the writing and subsequent revisions of
Understanding Poetry and Understanding Fiction. Warren also
offered an evening reading of his poetry. They were followed
in the spring by Bernard Malamud, who read stories and a
long selection from Dubin's Lives, which had just been
published. And at year's end, Eudora Welty came for a
reading followed the next day by a seminar sponsored by the
graduate students and the Creative Writing Program. The 1982
academic year began with a seminar on Melville in honor of
Nathalia Wright and featuring papers by Harrison Hayford,
editor of the Newberry Edition of Melville, and Donald
Yanella, executive secretary of the Melville Society, as
well as presentations by Allison Ensor, Marjorie Pryse, and
William Shurr of our own department. The 1983 year saw an
impressive writers' conference, "Southern Aspects," funded
by grants from the Better English Fund and the Tennessee
Committee for the Humanities. Better than seventy students
enrolled for the conference, which offered public readings
and discussions in the evenings by visiting writers George
Garrett, David Madden, Allen Wier, Richard Dillard, Malcolm
Glass, and Cathryn Hankla, as well as Robert Drake, Jon
Manchip White, and Alan Cheuse from our own faculty. During
the course of the year a number of poets visited the campus
as well: Robert Bly, Lawrence Lieberman, Carolyn Forche, and
Clayton Eshleman. In the spring of 1984, the Department and
the Better English Fund sponsored a symposium on recent
trends in Restoration and 18th Century scholarship, with
presentations from Aubrey Williams, Paul Hunter, and
Maximillian Novak. Visiting writers during 1984 and 1985
included Ronald Blythe, Audre Lorde, Nora Sayre, and Denise
Levertov. Among the distinguished scholars who have lectured

in recent years are John Fleming, Derek Pearsall, Charles Altieri, and Sir Steven Runciman. The Southern Writers Series which celebrated the opening of the new Hodges Library featured George Garrett, Alex Haley, Al Young, Wilma Dykeman, Lee Smith, Bobbie Ann Mason and Donald Justice.

CURRICULUM

Two significant developments in the 1980s resulted in significant changes not only in the English curriculum but also that of the College. At Dean Landen's direction, the College undertook a complete revision of the 1972 curriculum and implemented the revised curriculum in 1984. The revisions proceeded in the midst of a debate of several years' duration on switching the campus to the semester system in the fall of 1988. Although the 1984 curriculum is too extensive to be described in detail in these pages, it was characterized by a reemphasis on foreign languages and a return to a simpler and more cohesive set of requirements for fulfilling the distribution requirements in the Humanities, Natural Sciences, and Social Sciences. What some of its detractors called the Chinese Menu aspect of the 1972 curriculum ("choose any two courses from column A and any two from column B") was replaced by a smaller list of sequential courses in each of the three major areas--many of them specifically designed to enhance liberal learning at the lower division level. Writing emphasis courses were introduced at the sophomore and upper division levels, and additional distribution requirements in the upper division were added as well. Acknowledging the expansion of the interdisciplinary program in linguistics, the department dropped its own concentration in language and inserted a one-course language requirement into the concentrations in literature and in writing. The move to semesters witnessed the dropping of the three-optioned third quarter of freshman composition (literature, language, business and technical writing) in favor of a single two-semester sequence in which some of the material from the business and technical writing course was reintroduced into the first term and a fair amount of the language and literature courses added to the expanded second term. At this writing, the new sequence has yet to be taught, and the department is prepared to initiate revisions if and when they are needed.

At the graduate level, we dropped the Master of Arts in College Teaching, which few students were taking, and added an M.A. with writing emphasis which required students to take half of their coursework in literature but which also permitted substantial coursework and a thesis in creative, expository, or technical writing. Job placement for the first recipients of the degree has been high, and the prospects for continued success appear bright. The fact that doctoral students will take fewer courses on semesters than on quarters necessitated a reduction in the number of written preliminary examinations and allowed at the same time an extension of the length of time a student could devote to each.

THE PAST AND THE FUTURE

The past decade has been an exciting and a productive one. We are too close to it to evaluate it properly, and it would not be appropriate, in any case, for the present writers to attempt such an evaluation. A few promising statistics might, however, be noted. The Assessment of Research Doctoral Programs: Humanities (American Council of Education, 1982) ranked the UTK Department of English almost squarely in the middle of 104 departments which were evaluated. In the category of "Improvement over the past five years," however, we ranked 19th. There is hope that our peers' perception of us may continue to improve. The establishment by the Better English Fund of a sabbatical program should enable an already productive department to increase both the quality and the quantity of its scholarship. The most dramatic recent evidence of the value of the program was the appearance in 1985 (some two years after the program was implemented) of 13 books written or edited by members of the departmental faculty, almost all of whom had completed the book during the sabbatical. The statistics for the entire decade are almost equally impressive. Though reporting procedures for our two sources (the systems office report of Publications and Creative

Achievements and our own Tennessee English Newsletter)
differ slightly, it appears that over the past ten years
(1978 through 1987) members of the Department of English
have produced some 58 books (and have had several others
reprinted or appear in revised editions) and articles,
poems, stories, and reviews numbering nearly 600. Many of
these have elicited highly laudatory reviews from some of
the best scholars in the profession; some have brought
honors such as the National Book Award (to Richard Beale
Davis), the Starett Prize and the Poetry Society of
America's "best first book" award (to Arthur Smith), the
Keats-Shelley Association prize for best article of the year
(to Nancy Goslee), and the the Elliott Prize of the Medieval
Academy of America for best essay of the year in Medieval
Studies (to Thomas Heffernan). Participation in national
meetings is at an all-time high, and many members of the
department hold major offices in professional societies and
sit on Executive Committees of divisions of MLA. Four
colleagues have won the Chancellor's Research Scholar Award
during the decade (John Fisher, Norman Sanders, Richard
Kelly, and William Shurr), and three others have won the
National Alumni Association Teaching Award (B. J. Leggett,
Bain Stewart [for the second time] and Patsy Hammontree).
We continue to honor outstanding teaching by Assistant
Professors, Instructors, and Teaching Assistants and
Associates with our own John C. Hodges Prizes for Excellence
in Teaching. When Professor Dorothy Scura of Virginia
Commonwealth University assumes the Headship of the
Department of English in January of 1989, she will inherit a
department which continues its longstanding commitment to
excellence in teaching, in research and in service, and
hopes with the promise of additional resources to enhance
its reputation and its success in all three aspects of its
mission.

Students

Most of this narrative of English Studies at the University has been about presidents, deans, professors, instructors, but very little about the students. Since the students were the ones who took the courses and for whom the curriculum was designed, it may well be asked what some of these students achieved after their University days. Although the University had small enrollments during the nineteenth century, many early graduates distinguished themselves. Some became ministers, lawyers, or held public office, and for these a literary education would have been helpful in an age when the writing and delivering of speeches played an important role. William G. McAdoo, Jr., the son of Professor McAdoo, had a reputation as an orator before he left the University to embark on his distinguished career that included the posts of Secretary of the Treasury in the Wilson cabinet and a senatorship from California. He was also a strong contender for the presidential nomination of the Democratic party in the conventions of 1920 and 1924. His autobiography contains much information about the University and his own role in the literary societies. In the 1890s three students, active in the writing of the University Magazine, became productive writers: Edwin McAdoo Wiley's writing was mostly in the field of library science, but Norman H. Pitman was a writer of fiction, much of which he based upon his experiences as a teacher in China. J. Walker McSpadden was the prolific author of some fifty books in every field from travel and geography to biography and fiction, including a novel based upon the life of President Andrew Johnson. In the early twentieth century Joseph Wood Krutch, a pupil of Bruce, became a well-known writer and the winner of numerous awards, including a National Book Award. His frank criticisms of the University and Knoxville made him for many years persona non grata to many sensitive local persons, but there is no doubt that he is the best-known literary figure among the alumni.

Although James Maynard, son of Horace Maynard, of the class of 1872 never became a professional writer (he was a successful Knoxville business man, lawyer, trustee, and treasurer of the University) I noted that during the editorship of John B. Henneman of the Sewanee Review two essays from his pen were published: "John of Antioch, Saint Chrysostom" in 1904 and "Saint Martin of Tours" in 1906. It is not too fanciful to assume that the inclusion of these essays reflects not only his friendship with Henneman but also the literary ambience of the University at the turn of the century. Henneman also published in the Sewanee Review (1905) an essay by another alumnus and trustee, Joshua W. Caldwell: "A Brief for Boswell."

In my fifth chapter I mentioned that in the early 1950s Professor Daniel encouraged David Madden and Cormac McCarthy at the beginning of their successful careers as novelists. McCarthy received the William Faulkner Foundation Award in 1965 and the prestigious and valuable MacArthur Foundation Award in 1981. Robert Herring, who came much later as a graduate student and received an M.A., has received recognition for his novels set within the Appalachian region, especially for his novel Hub (1981).

An anthology of fiction by Tennessee writers, Homewords: A Book of Tennessee Writers (University of Tennessee Press, 1986) contains selections from several writers who either attended or graduated from the University. In addition to McCarthy, Madden, and Herring, selections by Marilou Awiakta, George Scarborough, and Jeff Daniel Marion are included. Madison Jones, who is also represented in the anthology was an instructor for one year in the Department in 1956.

Owen Davis, a native of the state of Maine, spent his freshman year at the University, and in 1923 received the Pulitzer Prize for drama for his play Ice-Bound. Bernadotte E. Schmitt, son of Dean Schmitt and a Rhodes Scholar, received the Pulitzer prize for history in 1931 for The Coming of the War: 1914. John M. Hightower, an Associated Press foreign correspondent and a U.T. alumnus, also received a Pulitzer Prize for International Reporting in 1952 for his coverage of events related to the Korean conflict.

Richard Marius, an historian, has published not only scholarly biographies of Luther and Sir Thomas More, but also two novels: The Coming of Rain (1969--a Book of the

Month Club Selection) and <u>Bound for the Promised Land</u> (1976). Marius has testified to his appreciation and high regard for his teacher of Freshman English--John Hansen. It is reassuring to observe that Freshman English does not necessarily destroy latent creative talent, but that some students actually thrive under the rigors of that often dreaded course!

Several of our M.A.s have had careers in fields other than English. Drake Bush has had a career in publishing with Harcourt, Brace, Jovanovitch; Kenneth Cherry as director of the University of Kentucky Press; Stephen Cox as director of the University of Nebraska Press. Jerrell P. Childress, after a few years of teaching, took a position at Sterchi's, where he later became a vice-president and tells me that he has written "volumes of instructions to employees and reports to stockholders" but questions their "literary merit"! Thomas Shaw, after a B.A. and M.A. in English, took a Ph.D. in Slavic Languages and Literature at Harvard, and has been a professor in that field at the University of Wisconsin at Madison and an authority on Pushkin.

Several M.A.s have held collegiate administrative posts: William Burks (M.A. 1956), chairman at Martin Methodist College, Pulaski, Tennessee; F. Mark Davis (M.A. 1958), Academic Vice President and Dean at Atlantic Christian College; Bob Gentry (M.A. 1966), chairman at the Kent Campus, Florida Junior College at Jacksonville. Frank Day, an M.A. from the 1950s, is a full professor at Clemson and the author of books on Empson and Koestler in the Twayne Series.

Our first Ph.D. was awarded in 1950, and since then two hundred and twenty-eight (228) have been awarded. I do not have information about the subsequent careers of all these, but a few names I can mention, and can only apologize for those omitted whom I should have included. At the end of this book there is a list of the recipients of the Ph.D.s in English.

Several of these have become for varying lengths of time department or division heads and directors of graduate programs:

J. Lasley Dameron: Memphis State University.

Jack Durant: (Director of Graduate Studies): North Carolina State.

Mary S. Weinkauf: Dakota Wesleyan.

Thomas Gasque: University of South Dakota.

Nancy Fisher: Roane State Community College.

Judy C. Brown: Clayton Junior College.

Paulina Buhl Noble: Shorter College.

Richard Cornelius: Bryan College.

Katherine James: Atlantic Christian College.

Robert Weathersby: Dalton Junior College.

Elena Zimmerman: Clayton Junior College.

John W. Warren: Tennessee Technological University.

Several have also become deans and vice-presidents:

Joseph M. Ernest, Jr.: Academic Vice-president, William Carey College.

Boyd Litzinger: Dean of Arts and Sciences, St. Bonaventure.

William C. Moran, Dean of Arts and Sciences, Winthrop College.

John W. Morris: Vice Chancellor for Academic Affairs, University of Wisconsin at Eau Claire.

Carolyn P. Blair: Dean, Maryville College.

James W. Mathews: West Georgia College.

Dean Cantrell: Berry College.

Florence Krause: William Woods College.

Carol McGinnis Kay: Dean of Humanities and Social Sciences, University of South Carolina. (Formerly Dean, Randolph-Macon Woman's College).

Two of the Department's Ph.D.s held the post of ADE (Association of Departments of English) Coordinators for the Modern Language Association: Jasper Neel and Elizabeth Wooten.

Not all of our Ph.D.s have pursued academic careers in English or academic administration, and I know of the following:

Michael Kelly: Director of Libraries, University of Texas at San Antonio.

Mary Q. Kelly: an attorney in San Antonio.

Sue Barnett Bohringer: an attorney in New York City.

Robert Dedmon: Episcopal Clergyman, St. Mark's Church, Nashville.

Donald Kay: Associate Vice-President for Development, University of South Carolina.

*Several students of English at the University who received
A.B. or M.A. degrees took a Ph.D. at other universities.
This list, by no means complete, lists a few:*

James R. Baird (B.A., M.A.) Yale

William Barnhart (M.A.) North Carolina

William W. Bass (M.A.) North Carolina

William Boone (B.A.) Rochester

Robert Carringer (A.B.) Indiana

Elizabeth Emerson (M.A.) Bryn Mawr

Allison R. Ensor (M.A.) Indiana

Judith Fisher (M.A.) Illinois

Theodore Huguelet (M.A.) North Carolina

James H. Justus (A.B., M.A.) Washington

Frank Kersnowski (A.B., M.A.) Kansas

Florence Marsh (M.A.) Yale

Eleanor Drake Mitchell (M.A.) Maryland

Michael Montgomery (M.A.) Florida

Veatrice Nelson (M.A.) Georgia State

Rupert Palmer (A.B., M.A.) Yale

Phil Phelps (M.A.) New Mexico

James Keith Robinson (B.A.) Harvard

Thomas Shaw (B.A., M.A.) Harvard

Barbara Wilkie Tedford (M.A.) Pittsburgh

Jac Tharpe (M.A.) Harvard

Julia Walker (M.A.) Purdue

Thomas Wheeler (M.A.) North Carolina

Edwin M. Wiley (B.A., M.A.) George Washington

Albert Wilhelm (B.A.) North Carolina

Offices and Secretaries

Before the 1940s the Department had no office, no secretary, and no telephone. Dr. Burke communicated with the small staff by brief notes which each person acknowledged by checking off his name and passing the notes on to the next person on the list. By the 1940s these informal arrangements no longer sufficed, and Hodges secured a small office, a telephone, and a secretary. Mrs. Mildred George served for about ten years from the early forties to 1951. Mrs. George was a pleasant receptionist, of cheerful disposition, who succeeded in keeping the faculty and graduate students in good humor, but unfortunately her secretarial skills were (in Hodges' view) not much more than adequate. Her successor, Miss Evelyn Hazen, a former high-school English teacher, who also knew French and Latin, was a perfect typist and ably handled the growing burden of administrative paper work with which Hodges and Knickerbocker were daily faced. She capably performed many time-consuming tasks such as annual reports, budgets, and the correspondence of the Head, but she seldom did any work for the staff. Where Mrs. George had been cheerful, amiable, and a good listener to the complaints of students and faculty, Miss Hazen had her own complaints to air. Of uncertain temper, she could explode, and the prudent learned to avoid the office at such times. Assistants in the office stayed relatively short periods of time. Rumors were that she carried a gun in her handbag, but since I never saw one, I cannot vouch for the accuracy of the report. Brash young instructors and teaching assistants were quickly put in their place. One anecdote will illustrate: one assistant, with all the self-confidence he had acquired as a captain in the army, went into the office and asked for some typing to be done for him, and received the brusque reply: "I don't work for the underlings around here." Miss Hazen was a woman of independent wealth, and after her death in June, 1987 (aged eighty-eight) it proved to be just about the million or two at which she had hinted with such remarks as "I could buy them all out." The job was her "window on the world" as one professor phrased it. Her successor, Mrs. Joyce Smith, stayed a few years, and was both cheerful and competent, only leaving to go to a better-paid job in an upper administrative office. The present head secretary, Mrs. Wanda Giles, who came in July, 1973, happily combines the good qualities of her predecessors as to efficiency, good humor, and patience, and supervises a small staff of five: Sandra Lewis, Dinah Brock, Norma Meredith, Donita Owings, and Rosemary Wheeler. These cheerful, competent, and accommodating secretaries have been with the Department for several years. The increased availability of secretarial assistance has been of inestimable benefit to the staff and to the departmental program.   In former days professors did most of their own typing at home.   After the Department moved to the McClung Tower, the graduate office became separate from the main office, and the secretary in that office tended exclusively to the correspondence and paper work with which the director and associate directors dealt.

The Hodges Lectures

Donald Davie. *Czeslaw Milosz and the Insufficiency of Lyric*. Knoxville: *University of Tennessee Press. 1986*.

William R. Gibson. *Theodore Roosevelt Among the Humorists: W. D. Howells, Mark Twain, and Mr. Dooley*. Knoxville: *University of Tennessee Press. 1980*.

Jean H. Hagstrum. *The Romantic Body: Love and Sexuality in Keats, Wordsworth, and Blake*. Knoxville: *University of Tennessee Press. 1985*.

Murray Krieger. *Arts on the Level: the Fall of the Elite Object*. Knoxville: *University of Tennessee Press. 1981*.

Ronald Paulson. *Book and Painting: Shakespeare, Milton, and the Bible: Literary Texts and the Emergence of English Painting*. Knoxville: *University of Tennessee Press. 1985*.

Fred C. Robinson. *Beowulf and the Appositive Style*. Knoxville: *University of Tennessee Press. 1985*.

Helen H. Vendler. *Wallace Stevens: Words Chosen Out of Desire*. Knoxville: *University of Tennessee Press. 1984*.

Bibliography

Chapter I. The Beginning to 1987

Stanley J. Folmsbee. Blount College and East Tennessee
College 1794-1840. University of Tennessee Record, 49:
No. 1. 1946. Reprinted: East Tennessee Historical
Society's Publications. No. 17. 1945.

Stanley J. Folmsbee. East Tennessee University 1840-1879:
Predecessor of the University of Tennessee. University
of Tennessee Record. 62: No. 3. 1959.

John Bell Henneman. "The Study of English in the South."
Sewanee Review II (1893-94), 180-97.

   An excellent survey of collegiate studies in English in
   the antebellum South.   This article has been very
   helpful in writing this chapter--especially since it was
   written by one of the University's own professors.

Charles Lee Lewis. Philander Priestley Claxton. Knoxville:
University of Tennessee Press. 1948.

William G. McAdoo, Jr. Crowded Years: The Reminiscences of
William G. McAdoo. Boston: Houghton Mifflin. 1931.

Neal O'Steen. "William G. McAdoo, Sr.,: A Man of Uncommon
Talents." Tennessee Alumnus, Summer 1984, pp. 3-5.

   "His respect for books and learning speak well for the
   kind of education being offered in Tennessee."

Neal O'Steen. "'Home to the Hill.'" Second Installment of
the life story of 19th century alumnus William G.
McAdoo, Sr." Tennessee Alumnus, Fall 1984, pp. 6-9.

Neal O'Steen. Tennessee Partners: The University of
Tennessee and Its Alumni Organization. Knoxville:
University of Tennessee National Alumni Association.
1986.   This history is not only of the alumni
organizations, but it also contains a well-written,

succinct account of the University's early years.

Neal O'Steen. "Edward Joynes: Scholar and Leader."
Tennessee Alumnus, Spring 1983, pp. 5-8.

The University Magazine. Conducted by the Senior Class of
East Tennessee University. 2 vols. I (1841-42); II
(1842-43). Both volumes are in Special Collections.
Vol. II has pencilled annotations by J. H. Martin
identifying the authors of several articles.

Special Collections of the University Library contains the
University's catalogs which began in 1838. These
catalogs are the principal source for information about
the staff and curriculum. The extensive McAdoo diaries
have been transcribed and are available in typescript.

Chapter II. English Under the Dabney Administration

Arthur B. Chitty. A Sewanee Sampler. Sewanee University
Press. 1978. Valuable for its information about
Professor Henneman.

T. C. Karns. "The University of Tennessee." Higher
Education in Tennessee, ed. Lucius S. Merriam.
Washington, D.C.: Government Printing Office. 1893.

Charles Lee Lewis. Philander Priestley Claxton. Knoxville:
University of Tennessee Press. 1948.

James Riley Montgomery. The Volunteer State Forges Its
University: The University of Tennessee, 1887-1919.
The University of Tennessee Record. 69: No. 6. 1966.

The best general account of the years--and the
constructive changes--covered in this chapter.

James Riley Montgomery. "Benton White's Recollections of
the University of Tennessee." East Tennessee Historical
Society's Publications. No. 33 (1961), pp. 79-96.

The University of Tennessee Magazine. 2 vols. 1894-95.
Copy in Special Collections.

Chapter III. English Under President Ayres
and James Douglas Bruce

"James Douglas Bruce Memorial." University of Tennessee
Record, 26: No.3. 1923.

> Contains a biographical memoir by Senator William Cabell
> Bruce; tributes by Hoskins, Burke, Judge Thornburgh, and
> James Maynard, a trustee and president of the Irving
> Club.

William Cabell Bruce. Recollections. Baltimore: Privately
printed. 1936.

> Only brief mention of J. D. Bruce. Extensive
> discussion of family relations and description of
> Staunton Hill in Charlotte County, Virginia, the
> plantation home of the Bruces.

George Herbert Clarke. Selected Poems. Ed. with Foreword
by George Whalley. General introduction by William O.
Raymond. Toronto: Ryerson Press, 1954. A volume in
the Ryerson Library of Canadian Poetry.

Charles Lee Lewis. Philander Priestley Claxton. Knoxville:
University of Tennessee Press. 1948.

Joseph Wood Krutch. More Lives Than One. New York:
William Sloane. 1962.

> The typescripts of this autobiography are in Special
> Collections (a gift solicited by Professor Hodges), but
> do not reveal significant differences from the published
> version.

John D. Margolis. Joseph Wood Krutch: A Writer's Life.
Knoxville: University of Tennessee Press. 1980.

James R. Montgomery. "Benton White's Recollections of the
University of Tennessee." East Tennessee Historical
Society's Publications, 33 (1961), 79-96.

Benton White was on campus 1901-04; 1907-10. A Chattanooga lawyer, White responded to a questionnaire Montgomery sent to alumni of that decade by returning a twenty-six page, highly entertaining account of student life and campus activity.

James R. Montgomery. The Volunteer State Forges Its University. The University of Tennessee Record. 69: No. 6. 1966.

The best general account for the years and events covered by this chapter as it also was for the preceding chapter.

William O. Raymond. "George Herbert Clarke." Proceedings and Transactions of the Royal Society of Canada, Third Series, 47 (1953), 69-74.

Reproduces a portrait of Clarke. Raymond's article is reprinted with minor changes in Queen's Quarterly, 60 (1953), of which Clarke had been a long-time editor and contributor.

Who Was Who has been useful for identifying many persons. The Dictionary of American Biography has articles on Dabney and Ayres.

James R. Montgomery has given me the following typescripts:

Herman Work. "Gold." A paper read before the Forum Club, Staunton, Va. 1962 (?). A reminiscence of Wolff.

Thomas R. Gilmore. Transcript of taped interview by Folmsbee and Montgomery. Brief reminiscences of Clarke and Burke.

The minutes of the board of Trustees for November 22, 1919. Special Collections.

Chapter IV: The Twenties: Growth and Change

Ellis F. Hartford. Our Common Mooring. Athens: University
of Georgia Press. 1941.

An account of Harcourt Morgan's work in behalf of
conservation in the South.

Joseph Wood Krutch. More Lives Than One. New York:
William Sloane. 1962.

John D. Margolis. Joseph Wood Krutch: A Writer's Life.
Knoxville: University of Tennessee Press. 1980.

Supplements Krutch's autobiography by quotations from
Krutch's journalistic writings about the Scopes trial
and his on-going "dialogue" with Knoxville and the
University.

James R. Montgomery. Threshold of a New Day. The
University of Tennessee 1919-1946. The University of
Tennessee Record. 74: No. 6. 1971.

The best general account of the University for these
years.

James R. Montgomery and Gerald Gaither. "Evolution and
Education in Tennessee: Decisions and Dilemmas."
Tennessee Historical Quarterly, 28 (Summer 1969), 141-
55.

The Scopes trial.

Neal O'Steen. Tennessee Partners: The University of
Tennessee and Its Alumni Organization. Knoxville: The
University of Tennessee National Alumni Association.
1986.

An informative account of the University's history
during these years and the role of the alumni in
promoting its interests. See Chapter Three: "An

Evolving Partnership, 1916-1948.

Mouzon Peters. "The Story of Dr. Harcourt A. Morgan." Book Five of <u>Makers of Millions Not for Themselves--But for You</u>. Tennessee Department of Agriculture. 1951. Pp. 1-89.

Alwin Thaler. <u>Ports and Happy Havens: An Autobiography</u>. Knoxville: Privately printed. 1974.

This autobiography, written after Thaler had turned eighty, concentrates upon his early life, family, and old friends. Several passages, however, have valuable pieces of information about the Department, the University, and persons within the University community. See especially pp. 177-78; 185-98; 204, 235.

Manuscript Sources: Special Collections.

President J. D. Hoskins, after his retirement in 1946, planned to write a history of the university and wrote a few sketches of persons connected with the earlier days. His three-page sketch of Kent, Bruce, and Burke has been used in this and earlier chapters. There are sketches of a few other faculty but none of other English faculty. A typescript of his history entitled "Service to the State: A History of the University of Tennessee 1794-1934" is labeled "Preliminary Draft" and readers are invited to write comments or additions on the blank pages (no one has). The history has no reference to the English Department and few references to any faculty. Hoskins records mostly changes in organization, buildings, trustees, new departments, and new programs. It contains much factual information, but the only "human interest" I noted was a reference to Hallowe'en pranks of students in the early 1900s.

Chapter V. Depression and War: 1930-1945

Annual Reports of the Department; 1936-37 through 1945-46.

The annual reports have made the collection of materials
for the later chapters infinitely easier.

Edwin C. Kirkland. "The English Laboratory." Tennessee
Alumnus, April, 1937.

James R. Montgomery. "Faculty and Academic Matters."
Threshold of a New Day. University of Tennessee
Record, 74: No. 6. 1971.

This readable chapter (pp. 133-87) tells the academic
reader most of what he is interested in knowing about
the University for these years.

Neal O'Steen. "Theatre at UT: Another Part of the Academic
Grove." Tennessee Alumnus, Summer 1980, pp. 28-31.

This highly informative--and entertaining--article
narrates the efforts of groups within and outside the
University to bring theatre to Knoxville and the campus
and to provide an opportunity for budding actors and
technical assistants to try their talents. Because the
Department did not commit itself to supporting play
production until later in this period of my history,
most of the material was outside its scope.

G. Allen Yeomans and Paul L. Soper. "The Theatre." Heart
of the Valley: A History of Knoxville, Tennessee, ed.
Lucile Deaderick. Knoxville: East Tennessee Historical
Society. 1971. Pp. 457-81.

Chapter VI. Post-War Growth: The Hodges Years: 1945-62

The Annual Reports for the years 1945-62.

> These reports give the fullest details and descriptions
> of the changes in the Department.

Lee S. Greene.   To Foster Knowledge.   Knoxville: The
University of Tennessee Press. 19.

> Greene's account of the origin and beginning of the
> Ph.D. programs at the University gives an outside view
> of what was going on.

Alwin Thaler.   Ports and Happy Havens.   Privately printed.
1974.

> Thaler, the first director of the Department's graduate
> program, gives a short account of the program's
> beginnings and a discreet reference to the opposition
> described by Greene.

Chapter VII. Increasing Numbers:
The Knickerbocker, Stewart and Fisher Years

The Annual Reports have provided most of the information in this chapter. When these were discontinued in 1974, the annual University of Tennessee English Newsletter took its place.

I have, in addition to the material in these reports, received statements about the programs in creative writing, black literature, language and linguistics, and English as a second language from Professors Jon White, R. Baxter Miller, Bethany Dumas, and Ilona Leki.

Some twenty-five responses to a letter mailed to former graduate students have given me valuable insights about the "old days." These have helped me to establish the atmosphere of the Department during those years and to provide me with a quotation or two.

Roster

The Roster lists not only those who in the early years were designated as instructors or professors of English but some who today might be considered as in "English." Before 1890 when President Dabney abolished the preparatory department, many professors, instructors, and lecturers did most of their teaching in the preparatory school. The appointment of the first Professor of Englsh was in 1867.

After 1920 the Roster does not attempt to be inclusive since at least two thousand persons have taught courses in English on the University's Knoxville campus. The list is, however, complete for those who achieved the rank of Associate or Full Professor and includes a few assistant professors and Ph.D. instructors who were in the Department for more than two or three years. Visiting Professors are included in a separate list. Omissions are inevitable, but are quite unintentional.

1838

Horace Maynard (A.B., Amherst). Tutor in preparatory department; 1843, Professor of Mathematics, Rhetoric and Belles-Lettres. For his later distinguished career see the Dictionary of American Biography.

1845

Rev. W. D. Carnes (M.A., U.T.). Professor of Ancient Languages and Belles-Lettres; principal of preparatory department. President of the University: 1858-60.

1867

Rev. Francis Mitchell Grace (M.A., U.T.). Professor of Rhetoric and English Literature. Went to Hiawssee College, where he became president. 1870.

1870

Richard Llewellyn Kirkpatrick (M.A., U.T.). Professor of English Language and Literature. In 1878 became Professor of History and Philosophy. Died. 1879.

1873

Rev. Thomas C. Teasdale, D.D. Professor of Rhetoric and Elocution. Resigned. 1877.

1877

William Gibbs McAdoo, Sr. (B.A., U.T.). Instructor in preparatory department; 1879: Instructor of English and History and Librarian; 1884: Adjunct Professor of English. Fired 1886. Died. 1894.

1878

Edward Southey Joynes (M.A., LL.D., Virginia). Professor of English Language and Belles-Lettres. Went to University of South Carolina as Professor of Modern Languages. 1882. Died. 1917.

1882

Rodes Massie (M.A., Virginia). Professor of English and Modern Languages. Fired by Dabney in 1887. Later career untraced.

1886

Thomas C. Karns (M.A., U.T.). Head of preparatory department.Associate Professor of English Language and Literature. 1888. Later Librarian and Associate Professor of History and Philosophy. Resigned. 1899.

1887

William Isaac Thomas (A.B., M.A., Ph.D., U.T.). Adjunct Professor of English and Modern Languages. Resigned. 1888. Died. 1947.

1888

Charles W. Kent (M.A., Virginia; Ph.D., Leipzig). Professor of English and Modern Languages. Went to University of Virginia. 1893. Died. 1917.

Kenneth G. Matheson (M.A., Stanford). Commandant of Cadets

and Assistant Professor of English. Resigned 1890.
Later Professor of English at Georgia Institute of
Technology and President (1922), Drexel Institute
(Philadelphia). Died. 1931.

1890

Edmund McMillan Davis. (B.A., U.T.). Fellow and Instructor
in English. First teaching Fellow. Resigned. 1892.

1893

John Bell Henneman. (M.A., Virginia, Ph.D., Berlin).
Professor of English Language and Literature. Went to
the University of the South. 1900. Died. 1908.

Joseph M. Black. (B.A., U.T.). Instructor in English and
Mathematics. Resigned. 1895. Later practiced law in
Knoxville.

1896

Norman Hinsdale Pitman. (M.A., U.T.). Instructor of
English. Resigned. 1898. Later taught at Peking
(China) Teachers College. Died. 1925.

1897

Edwin McAdoo Wiley. (M.A., U.T.). Instructor of English and
Librarian. Later a librarian at Vanderbilt and
Stanford. Ph.D. (George Washington University).
Died. 1924.

1899

Florence Skeffington. (M.A., Mary Sharp College).
Instructor and Assistant Professor of English. Dean of
Women. First woman faculty member. Resigned. 1905.

1900

James Douglas Bruce. (M.A., Virginia; Ph.D., Johns Hopkins).
Professor of English. Died. 1923.

1902

Emilie Watts McVea. (St. Mary's, Raleigh; A.B., M.A.,
   Columbia University). Instructor in the English
   Language and Literature. Taught in the Department of
   Education (P. P. Claxton, chairman). Went to University
   of Cincinnati. 1904. Later President of Sweet Briar
   College. Died. 1928.

1905

Samuel L. Wolff. (Harvard; M.A. and LL.B., Columbia
   University). Assistant Professor of English. Went to
   Columbia University. 1907.

1907

John Thompson Brown. (M.A., Virginia). Assistant Professor
   of English. Resigned. 1912.

1909

Charles Bell Burke. (Union, Cornell). Professor of English.
   Retired. 1942.

1911

George Herbert Clarke. (McMaster; honorary doctorates from
   McMaster, Bishop's, and Queen's College--Canada).
   Professor of English. Went to the University of the
   South. 1919.

1916

Frank M. Darnall. (M.A., Jefferson College; graduate study,
   U.T., Leipzig). Acting Professor of English. Resigned.
   1917.

1920

Allan H. Gilbert. (Harvard). Went to Duke University. 1921.

Mamie C. Johnston. (Tusculum; M.A., U.T.). Retired. 1949.

1921

John C. Hodges. (Harvard). Retired. 1962. Died. 1967.

1923

Alwin Thaler. (Adelphi, Harvard). Retired. 1961. Died. 1977.

1927

Roscoe E. Parker. (North Carolina, California at Berkeley). Retired. 1956. Died. 1984.

1929

John B. Emperor. (Cornell). Died. 1945.

1930

Edwin C. Kirkland. (Wofford, Northwestern). Went to University of Florida. 1946.

1934

John S. Davenport. (Cornell, North Carolina). Went to Knox College (Ill.). 1944.

Ralph L. Collins. (University of the South, Yale). Went to Indiana University, 1935, where he later became Vice-president and dean of the Faculties. Died. 1963.

Clarence C. Green (Harvard). Went to Lehigh. 1936.

1935

Bradford A. Booth. (Allegheny, Harvard). Went to UCLA. 1936. Later founded Nineteenth-Century Fiction. Died. 1968.

Kenneth Curry. (Rollins, Yale). Retired. 1978.

Rutherford B. Delmage. (St. Lawrence, Cornell). Went to St. Lawrence University. 1937.

Charles B. Woods. (Harvard). Went to University of Iowa. 1936.

1936

John J. Elson. (Cornell). Resigned in 1943. Went to Knoxville News-Sentinel.

Louis F. Peck. (Brown, Harvard). Went to Pennsylvania State. 1945.

Paul L. Soper. (Washington, Cornell). Moved as head to newly created Department of Speech and Theatre. 1968. Retired. 1976.

1937

E. Aubert Mooney, Jr. (Cornell). Resigned. 1939. Later went to University of Maryland.

1939

Charles R. Mangam. (Amherst, Cornell). Went to Tennessee Tech University, 1954. Later head of English Department at University of Tennessee, Martin.

Guy Simpson Miles. (Vanderbilt). Went to University of Florida. 1948.

1940

Bain Tate Stewart. (Vanderbilt, Northwestern). Retired. 1985.

1943

Maurice Baudin, Jr. (M.A., New York University). Went to

N.Y.U. 1946. A free-lance writer. Died (about) 1985.

1946

J. Frederick Fields (M.A., Ohio State). Went to Speech and Theatre. 1968.

Curtis Dahl. (Yale). Went to Wheaton College (MA). 1948.

Kenneth L. Knickerbocker. (Southern Methodist, Yale). Retired. 1974.

Clarence P. Lee. (Washington and Lee, Oxford University-- Rhodes Scholar). Resigned. 1956. Later went to Jacksonville University (FL).

F. DeWolfe Miller, III. (Davidson, Virginia). Retired. 1978.

Charles F. Webb. (Maryville; M.A., U.T.). Retired. 1970.

1947

Richard Beale Davis. (Randolph-Macon, Virginia). Retired. 1977. Died. 1981.

Robert W. Daniel. (University of the South, Yale). Went to Kenyon College. 1960. Died. 1984.

John A. Hansen, Jr. (Franklin and Marshall, Yale). Retired. 1978.

Robert L. Hickey. (Duke). Went to Tusculum College. 1966. Died (about) 1984.

1948

Percy G. Adams. (Texas College of Arts and Industries, Texas). Retired. 1985.

1949

Nathalia Wright. (Maryville, Yale). Retired. 1981.

1951

Russell E. Green. (South Carolina; M.F.A., Yale). Resigned. 1961. Went to Whittier College; in 1965 to University of South Carolina.

Kenneth D. Wright. (U.T., Ohio State). Resigned. 1958. Later associate vice-president, Div. of Continuing Education.

1953

Durant H. da Ponte. Went to Graduate Office as Assistant Dean. 1963. Died. 1964.

Albert M. Lyles. (Union College in N.Y.; Pennsylvania; Rutgers). Went to Virginia Commonwealth University. 1970. Later Dean of Winthrop College.

Alan M. Markman. (Michigan). Went to University of Pittsburgh. 1956.

Raymond C. Sutherland. (Transylvania, General Theological, Kentucky). Went to Georgia State University. 1957.

1955

Thomas V. Wheeler. (Maryville; U.T., M.A.; North Carolina).

1956

Frank A. Lester (U.T.). Later director of Television Services. Division of Continuing Education.

1957

Holger O. Nygard. (University of British Columbia, California at Berkeley). Went to Duke University. 1960.

1958

V. Carolyn Martin. (U.T.). Died. 1980.

1960

Eric Stockton (Northwestern, Harvard). Retired (ill health). 1970. Died. 1982.

Stephen L. Mooney. (Alabama, U.T.). Went to University of Tennessee, Martin. 1964.

Lorayne W. Lester. (Ed.D., U.T.). Moved to Department of Speech and Theatre 1968. Later was head of that Department.

1961

Thomas P. Cooke. (M.F.A., Yale). Moved to Department of Speech and Theatre. 1968.

George Thaddeus Wright. (Columbia, California at Berkeley). Went to University of Minnesota. 1968.

John D. Tinkler. (Vanderbilt; M.A., Florida; Stanford). Went to U.T., Chattanooga. 1973.

Jack E. Reese. (Berea, Kentucky). Went to Graduate Office as Assistant Dean. 1964. Became Chancellor, U.T., Knoxville, 1973.

1962

Norman J. Sanders. (Birmingham, Shakespeare Institute).

1963

Neil D. Isaacs. (Dartmouth, Brown). Went to University of Maryland. 1971.

Francelia Butler (Oberlin; M.A., Georgetown; Virginia). Went to University of Connecticut. 1965.

1964

Edward W. Bratton. (Arkansas, Illinois).

Samuel H. McMillan. (Southern Methodist, Texas). Resigned. 1976.

Ralph H. Walker. (Texas). Retired. 1987.

1965

Robert Y. Drake, Jr. (Vanderbilt, Yale).

Allison R. Ensor. (Tennessee Tech; M.A., U.T.; Indiana).

James E. Gill. (Texas, North Carolina).

Bobby J. Leggett. (Lambuth, Florida).

A. Richard Penner. (North Texas, Colorado).

1966

Max E. Cordonnier. (Park College, Kansas). Went to Southeast Missouri College. 1967.

Clark H. Rogers. Resigned. 1968.

1967

Patsy Hammontree. (U.T.)

Gail Compton. (Stetson, Florida). Went to Flagler College. 1974.

Albert J. Harris. (Ed.D., Tennessee). Moved to Department of Speech and Theatre. 1968.

Robert Lovejoy. (Western Reserve). Went to Carleton College. 1970.

1968

Lorraine S. Burghardt. (Chicago).

Chester T. Rebok. (M.A., Penn State). Resigned. 1972.

1969

D. Allen Carroll. (Wake Forest, North Carolina).

James J. Foster. (Johns Hopkins, Duke). Went to University of Maryland, Baltimore). 1975.

Frank K. Robinson. (Texas).

1970

Barry J. Gaines. (Rice, Wisconsin). Went to University of New Mexico. 1980.

David F. Goslee, (Oberlin, Yale).

Nancy M. Goslee. (Smith, Yale).

1971

Mary P. Richards. (Southern Methodist, Wisconsin). Has served as associate graduate dean and associate dean of the college of liberal arts (1986-87). Went to Auburn (1988) as Dean of Liberal Arts.

Richard T. Goode (Washington and Lee, Texas). Went to Queen's. 1978.

James Koger. (University of the South, Rice). Went to Birmingham Southern. 1976. Later Lynchburg College.

David Kwinn. (Cornell). Resigned. 1973.

Paul Merchant. (Cambridge, Shakespeare Institute). Went to University of Warwick, Coventry. 1973.

1972

John H. Fisher. (Maryville, Pennsylvania). First John C. Hodges Professor of English.

1974

Bethany Dumas. (Lamar State, Arkansas).

1975

Michael Lofaro, (Rensselaer Polytechnic, Maryland).

Thomas J. Heffernan. (Manhattan, N.Y.U., Cambridge).

Don R. Cox. (Wichita State, Missouri).

Jack M. Armistead. (Michigan State, Duke).

1976

Dale Myers. (Hendrix, Florida). Became head of English Foreign Language Institute, U.T.

Ilona Leki. (Illinois).

1977

Jon Manchip White. (St. Catherine's College, Cambridge).

R. Baxter Miller. (North Carolina Central, Brown).

Daniel J. Schneider. (Chicago, Northwestern).

1978

Joseph B. Trahern, Jr. (Vanderbilt, Princeton).

Marjorie Pryse. (Ohio State, California--Santa Cruz). Resigned. 1987.

Charles J. Maland. (Augsburg, Michigan).

1981

Michael Keene. (Texas).

Dorothy Denniston. (Simmons, Northeastern, Brown). Went to Brown.   1987.

Marilyn Kallet. (Rutgers).

Kate Adams. (North Carolina, Florida State). Went to Loyola University. 1987.

William J. Shurr. (Loyola, North Carolina).

1982

Robert Stillman. (New College in Florida, Pennsylvania).

George Hutchinson. (Brown, Indiana).

Stephen Watt. (Illinois). Went to Indiana University. 1985.

1985

Allen Dunn. (UCLA, Washington).

Donald Samson. (Cornell, North Carolina).

John Zomchick. (Penn State, Columbia).

1986

Kathryn Riley. (Georgia State, Louisana State University, Maryland).

Jeanie Forte. (Reed College, San Francisco State, Washington).

Arthur Smith. (San Francisco State, Houston University).

Linda Bensel-Meyers (Chicago, Oregon).

1987

Ray Wallace. (Eastern Illinois, Illinois State University).

1988

Richard J. Finneran. (New York University, University of North Carolina at Chapel Hill).

Mary E. Papke. (University of Illinois at Champaign-Urbana, McGill University).

Dorothy M. Scura. (Louisiana State University, Teachers College-Columbia University, University of North Carolina at Chapel Hill).

Publications

This list contains only <u>books</u> published by the English staff during their tenure at the University. It does not include books published by professors before or after their stay at the University. I have included textbooks since many of these have considerable importance for the Department, most notably John C. Hodges' <u>Harbrace College Handbook</u>. I have also included volumes of poetry and fiction. I have excluded pamphlets and ephemeral publications chiefly associated with University affairs. Since many of the professorial staff have written important articles in well-known scholarly journals, the list does not completely reflect the scholarly interests and achievements of the Department. I hope that I have included every title, but I may have overlooked a few that I should have discovered.

1889

Charles W. Kent, ed. <u>Elene</u>. (Notes, Vocabulary, and Introduction). Ginn and Co.

1903

James Douglas Bruce, ed. <u>Le Morte Arthur</u>..re-edited from <u>MS. Harley 2252</u>. Early English Text Society Publications. Vol. 88.

1914

George Herbert Clarke. <u>At the Shrine</u>. Stewart and Kidd. (Cincinnati).

1922

Alwin Thaler. <u>Shakespere</u> [sic] <u>to Sheridan: A Book About the Theatre of Yesterday and To-Day</u>. Harvard University Press.

1923

James Douglas Bruce. <u>Evolution of Arthurian Romance</u>. Johns

Hopkins Press.

1928

John B. Emperor. The Catullian Influence in English Lyric Poetry. 1600-1800. University of Missouri Studies. Vol. III. No. 3

Roscoe E. Parker. The Middle English Stanzaic Versions of the Life of Saint Anne. Early English Text Society for Humphrey Milford, Oxford University Press.

1929

Alwin Thaler. Shakspere's [sic] Silences. Harvard University Press.

1933

Roscoe E. Parker (with H. W. Robbins). Advanced Composition. Prentice-Hall.

1936

Alwin Thaler, ed. (with C. M. Gayley). Representative English Comedies. Vol. IV. Macmillan.

1937

Roscoe E. Parker. The Principles and Practice of Teaching English. Prentice-Hall.

1941

John C. Hodges. William Congreve, the Man. Modern Language Association and Oxford University Press.

John C. Hodges. The Harbrace Handbook of English. (Later editions published as Harbrace College Handbook). Harcourt, Brace.

Alwin Thaler. Shakespeare and Democracy. University of

Tennessee Press.

1942

John C. Hodges. The Harbrace Omnibus. Harcourt, Brace.

1943

John C. Hodges. Basic Writing and Reading. Harcourt, Brace.

1946

John C. Hodges. English Manual for Teachers. State Department of Education (Nashville).

Roscoe E. Parker, ed. Studies of Higher Education in the South. Committee on Work Conferences on Higher Education of Southern Association of Schools and Colleges.

1947

Alwin Thaler. Shakespeare and Sir Philip Sidney. Harvard University Press.

1949

Paul L. Soper. Basic Public Speaking. Oxford University Press (New York).

Nathalia Wright. Melville's Use of the Bible. Duke University Press.

Robert Daniel. Introduction to Jane Austen, Pride and Prejudice. Rinehart.

1950

Kenneth L. Knickerbocker, ed. (with W. C. DeVane) New Letters of Robert Browning. Yale University Press.

1951

Kenneth L. Knickerbocker, ed. <u>Selected Poetry of Robert Browning</u>. Random House.

Kenneth L. Knickerbocker, ed. <u>Ideas for Writing: Readings for College Composition</u>. Henry Holt.

F. DeWolfe Miller, III. <u>Christopher Pearse Cranch and His Transcendental Cartoons</u>. Harvard University Press.

1952

Richard B. Davis, ed. <u>Chivers' Life of Poe</u>. E. P. Dutton.

John C. Hodges (with J. Hooper Wise and others). <u>College English: The First Year</u>. Harcourt, Brace.

1954

Richard B. Davis, ed. <u>Jeffersonian America: Notes on the United States of America; Collected in the Years 1805-6-7 and 11-12 by Sir Augustus John Foster</u>. Henry E. Huntington Library.

1955

Robert Daniel. (with Monroe Beardsley), ed. <u>Theme and Form: An Introduction to Literature</u>. Prentice-Hall.

Richard B. Davis. <u>George Sandys, Poet-Adventurer</u>. Columbia University Press and Bodley Head (London).

Richard B. Davis. <u>The Abbé Correa in America, 1802-1829</u>. American Philosophical Society.

Kenneth L. Knickerbocker, (with H. W. Reninger), ed. <u>Interpreting Literature</u>. Holt, Rinehart, and Winston.

1956

John C. Hodges. <u>The Library of William Congreve</u>. New York

Public Library.

1958

Nathalia Wright. Introduction to Horatio Greenough. The Travels, Observations, and Experience of a Yankee Stonecutter. Scholars' Facsimiles and Reprints (Gainesville, Fla.)

1959

F. DeWolfe Miller, III. ed. Walt Whitman's Drum-Taps (1865) and Sequel to Drum-Traps (1865-6). Scholars' Facsimiles and Reprints (Gainesville, Fla.).

1960

George T. Wright. The Poet in the Poem: the Personae of Eliot, Yeats, and Pound. University of California Press.

1961

Percy G. Adams. Translation with Introduction and Notes. Crevecoeur's Eighteenth-Century Travels in Pennsylvania and New York. University of Kentucky Press.

John L. Lievsay. Stefan Guazzo and the English Renaissance. University of North Carolina Press.

Bain T. Stewart, (with K. L. Knickerbocker), ed. Readings and Assignments: A Practical Approach to College Writing. Holt, Rinehart, and Winston.

Nathalia Wright, ed. John Galt's Life of Benjamin West. Scholars' Facsimiles and Reprints (Gainesville, Fla.).

1962

Percy G. Adams. Travelers and Travel Liars--1660-1800. University of California Press.

Eric W. Stockton. <u>The Major Latin Works of John Gower</u>. Translated with an Introduction and Notes. University of Washington Press.

1963

Richard B. Davis, ed. <u>William Fitzhugh and His Chesapeake World, 1676-1701</u>. University of North Carolina Press.

Francelia Butler. <u>The Skip Rope Book</u>. Dial Press.

Neil D. Isaacs (with Louis H. Leiter). <u>Approaches to the Short Story</u>. Chandler Publishing Co.

1964

John C. Hodges. <u>William Congreve: Letters and Documents</u>. Harcourt, Brace, and World.

1965

Kenneth Curry, ed. <u>New Letters of Robert Southey</u>. 2 vols. Columbia University Press.

Robert Drake. <u>Amazing Grace</u>. Chilton Books.

Kenneth L. Knickerbocker (with Boyd Litzinger), ed. <u>The Browning Critics</u>. University of Kentucky Press.

Norman Sanders. <u>William Shakespeare, Comedian</u>. Ohio English Association. Pamphlet No. 1.

Nathalia Wright. <u>American Novelists in Italy: The Discoverers: Allston to James</u>. University of Pennsylvania Press.

1966

Robert Drake. <u>Flannery O'Connor</u>. Eerdmans. Contemporary Writers in Christian Perspectives Series.

Stephen L. Mooney. News from the South: Poems. University of Tennessee Press.

Alwin Thaler. Shakespeare and Our World. University of Tennessee Press.

1967

Richard B. Davis. The Colonial Virginia Satirist: Mid-Eighteenth Commentaries on Politics, Religion, and Society. American Philosophical Society.

Bain T. Stewart (with K. L. Knickerbocker). Writing about Poetry. Holt, Rinehart, and Winston.

Nathalia Wright, ed. with Introduction. Washington Allston. Lectures on Art and Poems (1850) and Monaldi (1841). Scholars' Facsimiles and Reprints.

1968

Neil D. Isaacs. Structural Principles in Old English Poetry. University of Tennessee Press.

Neil D. Isaacs. (with Rose A. Zimbardo), ed. Tolkien and the Critics. University of Notre Dame Press.

Richard M. Kelly. The Night of Noah. Tennessee Poetry Press.

Samuel H. McMillan. The Poet in His World: Twelve in Tennessee. Tennessee Poetry Press.

Stephen L. Mooney. The Grave of the Dwarf, Irish Sketches, 1949-50. Dolmen Press. (Dublin).

Norman J. Sanders., ed. Two Gentlemen of Verona. Penguin Books.

1969

Richard B. Davis. American Literature through Bryant.

Goldentree Bibliographies. Appleton-Century-Crofts.

Allison R. Ensor. Mark Twain and the Bible. University of Kentucky Press.

1970

Richard B. Davis, ed. Letters of the British Spy by William Wirt. University of North Carolina Press.

Richard B. Davis (with C. Hugh Holman and Louis Rubin, Jr.), ed. Southern American Writing. Odyssey Press.

Richard M. Kelly, ed. with Introduction. The Best of Mr. Punch: The Humorous Writings of Douglas Jerrold. University of Tennessee Press.

Bobby J. Leggett. Housman's Land of Lost Content: A Critical Study of a Shropshire Lad. University of Tennessee Press.

Albert M. Lyles (with John Dobson). The John C. Hodges Collection of William Congreve. University of Tennessee Library.

Norman J. Sanders, ed. Richard II. Blackfriars Shakespeare. William C. Brown.

Norman J. Sanders, ed. Robert Greene's James the Fourth. Methuen (London) and Barnes and Noble.

Nathalia Wright. Introduction to Mary N. Murfree. In the Tennessee Mountains. Tennesseana Editions. University of Tennessee Press.

1971

Robert Drake. The Single Heart. Aurora Publishers (Nashville).

Harold Orton. Survey of English Dialects: Basic Material. Vols. II and III. E. J. Arnold and Sons (Leeds,

England).

Frank K. Robinson. <u>Edgar Lee Masters: An Exhibition in Commemoration of the Centenary of His Birth...Catalogue and Checklist of Books</u>. University of Texas Humanities Center.

1972

Percy G. Adams. Introduction. <u>The Exploration of Captain James Cook in the Pacific</u>. Dover Publications.

Lorraine S. Burghardt., ed. <u>Dialectology: Problems and Perspectives.</u> University of Tennessee Press.

Richard M. Kelly. <u>Douglas Jerrold</u>. Twayne Publishers.

A. Richard Penner. <u>Alan Sillitoe</u>. Twayne Publishers.

Nathalia Wright (with Harold Orton). <u>Questionnaire for the Investigation of American Regional English</u>. University of Tennessee Press.

Nathalia Wright, ed. <u>Letters of Horatio Greenough, American Sculptor</u>. University of Wisconsin Press.

1973

Richard B. Davis. <u>Literature and Society in Early Virginia 1608-1640</u>. Louisiana State University Press.

Alan R. Thomas. <u>The Linguistic Geography of Wales</u>. University of Wales Press.

Thomas V. Wheeler. <u>Paradise Lost and the Modern Reader</u>. University of Georgia Press.

1974

D. Allen Carroll, ed. Everard Guilpin's <u>Skialetheia, or a Shadow of Truth in Certain Epigrams.</u> University of North Carolina Press.

Bethany K. Dumas. E. E. Cummings: A Remembrance of Miracles. Vision Press and Barnes and Noble.

Harold Orton (with Nathalia Wright) A Word Geography of England. Seminar Press.

Alwin Thaler. Ports and Happy Havens. University of Tennessee English Department.

1975

Kenneth Curry. Southey. Routledge Author Guide Series. Routledge and Kegan Paul.

Robert Drake. The Burning Bush. Aurora Press (Nashville).

1976

Robert Drake. Introduction to Frances Boyd Calhoun. Miss Minerva and William Green Hill. Tennessee Editions Series. University of Tennessee Press.

1977

Percy G. Adams. Graces of Harmony: Alliteration, Assonance, Consonance in Eighteenth-Century Poetry. University of Georgia Press.

Kenneth Curry. Robert Southey: A Reference Guide. G. K. Hall.

Kenneth Curry. Sir Walter Scott's Edinburgh Annual Register. University of Tennessee Press.

Richard B. Davis. Intellectual Life in the Colonial South. 1585-1763. Three vols. University of Tennessee Press. Received National Book Award from the Association of American Publishers.

John H. Fisher, ed. The Complete Prose and Poetry of

Geoffrey Chaucer. Holt, Rinehart.

Frank K. Robinson, ed. The Harmony of Inner Music: Posthumous Poems of Edgar Lee Masters. University of Texas Press.

Jon M. White, ed. The Discovery of the Tomb of Tutankhamen. Dover Publications.

Nathalia Wright, ed. Washington Irving Journals and Notebooks. Vol. I. University of Wisconsin Press.

1978

Richard M. Kelly. Lewis Carroll. G. K. Hall and Twayne Publishers.

B. J. Leggett. The Poetic Art of A. E. Housman: Theory and Practice. University of Nebraska Press.

Michael A. Lofaro. The Life and Adventures of Daniel Boone. Lexington: University of Kentucky Press.

R. Baxter Miller. Langston Hughes and Gwendolyn Brooks: A Reference Guide. G. K. Hall.

Daniel J. Schneider. The Crystal Cage: Adventures of the Imagination in the Fiction of Henry James. Regents Press of Kansas.

1979

Percy G. Adams, ed. The Plays of James Thomson. Garland.

Jack M. Armistead. Nathaniel Lee. G. K. Hall.

Richard B. Davis. A Colonial Southern Bookshelf: Reading in the Eighteenth Century. Mercer University Lamar Memorial Lectures, No. 21. University of Georgia Press.

Marjorie Pryse. The Mark and the Knowledge: Social Stigma in Classic American Fiction. Ohio State University

Press.

Jon M. White. <u>Everyday Life of the North American Indian</u>. Batsford.

1980

Robert Drake. <u>The Home Place: A Memory and a Celebration</u>. Memphis State University Press.

A. Richard Penner. <u>Fiction of the Absurd: Pratfalls in the Void</u>. New American Library.

1981

Richard M. Kelly, ed. (with Stanley Appelbaum). <u>Great Cartoonists of Nineteenth-Century Punch</u>. Dover Publications.

Richard M. Kelly. <u>The Andy Griffith Show</u>. John F. Blair (Winston-Salem).

Charles J. Maland. <u>Frank Capra</u>. Twayne Publishers.

R. Baxter Miller, ed. <u>Black American Literature and Humanism</u>. University of Kentucky Press.

Marjorie Pryse. Introduction to Sarah O. Jewett's <u>The Country of the Pointed Firs</u>. W. W. Norton.

William H. Shurr. <u>Rappaccini's Children: American Writers in a Calvinist World</u>. University of Kentucky Press.

1982

Allison Ensor. <u>A Connecticut Yankee in King Arthur's Court</u>. A Norton Critical Edition. Norton.

Jon M. White. <u>Death by Dreaming</u>. Applewood Books (1981); Ace Books (New York).

1983

Percy G. Adams. <u>Travel Literature and the Evolution of the Novel</u>. University of Kentucky Press.

Richard M. Kelly. <u>George Du Maurier</u>. G. K. Hall.

Marjorie L. Pryse, ed. <u>Selected Stories of Sarah Orne Jewett</u>. W. W. Norton.

Norman J. Sanders, ed. <u>Henry VI, Parts I, II, and III</u>. New Penguin Shakespeare.

William H. Shurr. <u>The Marriage of Emily Dickinson: A Study of the Fascicles</u>. University of Kentucky Press.

1984

Don R. Cox, ed. (with W. S. Anderson). <u>The Technical Reader: Readings in Technical, Business and Scientific Communication</u>. Second edition. Holt, Rinehart, and Winston.

Kenneth Curry. <u>Robert Southey's Contributions to the Morning Post</u>. University of Alabama Press.

John H. Fisher (with Malcolm Richardson and Jane Fisher). <u>An Anthology of Chancery English</u>. University of Tennessee Press.

Richard M. Kelly. <u>Graham Greene</u>. Frederick Ungar.

Norman J. Sanders, ed. <u>Othello</u>. The New Cambridge Shakespeare.

Daniel J. Schneider. <u>D. H. Lawrence: The Artist as Pyschologist</u>. University of Kansas Press.

1985

Edward W. Bratton, (with B. J. Leggett, K. L. Knickerbocker, H. W. Reninger), ed. <u>Interpreting Literature</u>. Seventh

Edition. Holt, Rinehart, and Winston.

Don R. Cox. Arthur Conan Doyle. Frederick Ungar.

Nancy Goslee. Uriel's Eye: Miltonic Stationing and
Statuary in Blake, Keats, and Shelley. University of
Alabama Press.

Patsy G. Hammontree. Elvis Presley: A Bio-Bibliography.
Greenwood Press.

Marilyn Kallet. Honest Simplicity in William Carlos
Williams' "Asphodel: That Greeny Flower." Louisiana
State University Press.

Michael A. Lofaro, ed. Davy Crockett: The Man, The Legend,
The Legacy (1786-1986). University of Tennessee Press.

Marjorie Pryse (with Hortense Spillers). Conjuring: Black
Women, Fiction, and Literary Tradition. Indiana
University Press.

Thomas Wheeler. The Merchant of Venice: An Annotated
Bibliography. Garland Press.

Jon M. White. The Last Grand Master: A Novel of
Revolution. Vermont Countryman Press.

1986

D. Allen Carroll. A Midsummer Night's Dream: An Annotated
Bibliography. Garland.

Wynn J. Curtis (with Sheila Y. Graham). Harbrace ESL
Workbook. Harcourt, Brace, Jovanovich.

George B. Hutchinson. The Ecstatic Whitman: Literary
Shamanism and the Crisis of the Union. Ohio State
University Press.

Daniel J. Schneider. The Consciousness of D. H. Lawrence:
An Intellectual Biography. University Press of Kansas.

Merikay Waldvogel (with Bets Ramsey). The Quilts of Tennessee: Images of Domestic Life Prior to 1930. Rutledge Hill Press (Nashville).

Jon M. White. Contemporary Authors Autobiography Series. Gale Research Co.

[176]

Doctoral Dissertations
1950 - 1988

Aderholt, Martha Jo. "The Role of the Plain Folk in the Southern Antebellum Novel," (F. D. Miller). 1978.

Addison, James Clyde, Jr. "An Old-Spelling Critical Edition of Thomas Lodge's A Margarite of America (1596)," (Sanders). 1980.

Adler, Brian U. "Liberty and the Strongest Bonds: Fathers and Sons in Selected Short Works of Bernard Malamud," (Shurr). 1988.

Aiken, Gail Elizabeth. "This Accidental World: The Philosophy and Fiction of Iris Murdoch," (Sanders). 1979.

Andrews, Donald Frank. "The American Whig Review, 1845-1852." (Wright). 1977.

Attrey, Roshan L. "The Function of Oriental Allusions in James Joyce's Ulysses," (Schneider). 1986.

Austin, Marvin Fraley, Jr. "The Novels of Kurt Vonnegut, Jr.: A Confrontation with the Modern World," (Penner). 1975.

Bailey, Frederick. "The Historical Ballad: Its Tradition in Britain and America," (Stockton). 1963.

Bailey, Guy H., III. "Folk Speech on the Cumberland Plateau: A Phonological Analysis," (Dumas). 1979.

Bakker, Jan. "The Pastoral Design in the Southern Antebellum Novel," (Davis). 1975.

Ball, Jerry L. "Joseph of Arimathea and the Arthurian Tradition," (Richards). 1986.

Ballard, Sandra. "Harriette Simpson Arnow's Central Novel: Hunter's Horn. (Shurr). 1987.

[177]

Banks, Wallace Landrum. "The Imagery of Dryden's Rhymed Heroic Drama," (Lyles). 1967.

Barfield, Rayford Elliott, Jr. "Human Fecundity in Shakespearean Comedy with a Survey Chapter on the Histories and the Tragedies," (Sanders). 1969.

Barker, Mary Traylor. "Addison, A Librettist, and his Aesthetic of Opera," (Adams). 1977.

Barnett, William Joseph. "Redeemed Time: The Sacramental Vision and the Implicit Covenant in the Major Fiction of Richard Wright," (R. B. Miller). 1981.

Barr, George T. "The Ordinary World of Horton Foote," (Maland). 1986.

Baughn, Susan Leigh. "Wallace Stevens and the Idea of Language," (Leggett). 1983.

Beauchamp, J. Steven. "The Quest for the Hero in Browning's Early Poems, His Plays, and The Ring and the Book. (Kelly). 1987.

Beck, Charlotte Hudgens. "The Dramatic Mode in the Poetry of Randall Jarrell," (Kelly). 1972.

Benson, Ann (Thornton). "The American Criticism of Franz Kafka 1930-1948," (Daniel). 1958.

Berger, Harold Lynde. "Anti-Utopian Science Fiction of the Mid-Twentieth Century," (Penner). 1970.

Berry, David Chapman, Jr. "The Orphic and Narcissistic Themes in the Poetry and Criticism of James Dickey, 1951-1970," (Leggett). 1973.

Blackburn, John M. "An Old Spelling, Critical Edition of John Ford's The Lover's Melancholy," (Sanders). 1986.

Blair, Carolyn L. "Robert Browning as a Literary Critic," (Knickerbocker). 1961.

Bloy, Barbara. "The Woman Persona in Poetic Miscellanies of Elizabeth's Reign," (Sanders). 1977.

Blumenfeld, Jacob P. "Conventions and Modern Poetry: A Study in the Develoment of Period Mannerisms," (Daniel). 1957

Bohringer, Carol Sue Barnett. "'In so Far as We Have to Look Forward to Death as a Fact': A Study of W. H. Auden's Attitude Toward Time," (Leggett). 1976.

Bohringer, Kenneth Charles. "A Comparative Biographical Dictionary of Historical Characters in Ten Non-Shakespearean English History Plays of the Renaissance," (Sanders). 1973.

Bowers, Bege Kay. "Lawyers on Trial: Attitudes Toward the Lawyer's Use and Abuse of Rhetoric in Nineteenth-Century England," (Fisher). 1984.

Braymer, John. "The Literary Biographers of John Forster," (Kelly). 1977.

Braymer, Meta. "Satire and Comedy in Eighteenth-Century American Drama," (Davis). 1977.

Brogan, Katherine Mary Dougherty. "The Religious and Moral Poetry in the Elizabethan Miscellanies," (Stewart). 1979.

Bryant, Herbert. "The Relationship Between Defoe the Journalist and Defoe the Novelist," (Adams). 1973.

Buhl, Paulina Estella. "A Historical and Critical Study of Browning's Asolando Volume," (Knickerbocker). 1961.

Burton, Linda K. "An Anthology of Tennessee Short Fiction," (Ensor). 1981.

Busby, Bruce Stanley. "Browning the Biographer: An Exploration of Robert Browning's Interest in the Art of

Biography." (Kelly). 1976.

Butts, Leonard C. "Nature in the Selected Works of Four Contemporary American Novelists," (Schneider). 1979.

Cantrell, Dorothy Dean. "The Twentieth-Century Criticisms of Jane Austen's Mansfield and Emma," (Lyles). 1970.

Castles, William Henry, Jr. "The Virginia Gazette, 1736-1766: Its Editors, Editorial Policies, and Literary Content," (Davis). 1962.

Chamberlin, Mallory, Jr. "The World and the Child, Otherwise Called Mundus et Infans: A Critical Edition," (Sanders). 1969.

Chappell, Diane Landry. "The Selection of Emily Dickinson's Poems in College Textbook Anthologies, 1890-1976, (F. D. Miller). 1979.

Chastain, Carl Robert, Jr. "Matthew Arnold's Tragic Muse," (Kelly). 1973.

Cheatham, George Dayton. "An Old-Spelling, Critical Edition of William Rowley's "A New Wonder, A Woman Never Vext," (Sanders). 1982.

Churchman, Charles Johnston. "Samuel Davies: Representative Eighteenth-Century Poet," (Davis). 1973.

Clark, Ann R. "The Influence of Pietism on John Wesley as Revealed in His Journal," (Adams). 1986.

Considine, Raymond Howard. "Malcolm Lowry's Major Prose Fiction." (Penner). 1972.

Cornelius, Richard Meredith. "Christopher Marlowe's Use of the Bible," (Stewart). 1971.

Crafton, John M. "A Critical Old-Spelling Edition of Thomas Wilson's The Arte of Rhetorique (1553)," (Sanders). 1985.

Craven, Delle. "Mary E. Moragne: Her Journal and Its Environment; A Study in Upper South Carolina Culture," (Davis). 1952.

Dameron, John Lasley. "Edgar Allan Poe in the Mid-twentieth Century: His Literary Reputation in England and America 1928-1960 and a Bibliography of Poe Criticism, 1942-1960," (Davis). 1962.

Davis, Marijane R. "The Fascination of Knowledge": Imagistic Clues to the Labyrinth of Ambiguity in Henry James's The Golden Bowl. (Schneider). 1986.

Dawson, William Roy, Jr. "A Critical Edition of Thomas Middleton's A Trick to Catch the Old One," (Sanders). 1969.

Dedmon, Robert A. Jr. "The Contributions of Robert Southey to The Quarterly Review, 1809-1839," (Curry). 1975.

Dillard, Nancy Frey. "The English Fabular Tradition: Chaucer, Spenser, Dryden," (Stewart). 1973.

Dooley, Reinhold James. "Herman Melville's Short Fiction: Ideology and the American Confidence Game. (Shurr) 1988.

Dowell, Paul Wilson. "Vestiges of Rule Ritual in the Matter of England Romances," (Isaacs). 1971.

Duckworth, Phyllis Harris. "Naturalism and Romanticism in the Novels of George Moore," (Kelly). 1972.

Duke, Loraine (Hartmann). "Crime, Law, and Prison Experience in the Novels of Tobias Smollett," (Lyles). 1970.

Durant, Jack D. "The Imagery in Swift's Prose: A Descriptive Analysis of Forms and Functions," (Adams). 1963.

Duval, Elaine I. "Theatre and the Double: Revolutionary

Consciousness in Baraka and Artaud. (R. B. Miller). 1988.

Eckhart, Mary E. "A Thirteenth-Century Sermon Cycle in Oxford, Bodlean MS 471, Patr II. (Richards). 1987.

Edwards, Lawrence. "The Letters of Jacob Tonson," (Hodges). 1956.

Elder, Gaye Elisa. "Henry Adams on the American Presidency," (Wright). 1981.

Ellertsen, Edwin Peter. "The Idea of Limited Government in English History Plays During the Reign of Elizabeth I, 1558-1603," (Sanders). 1975.

Elliot, Norbert Louis, III. "Allegory in the Novels of Isaac Bashevis Singer," (Schneider). 1981.

Ensley, Helen Oliver. "The Rhythm of Poe's Poetry," (Davis). 1971.

Ernest, Joseph M. "Whittier and the American Writers," (Davis and Thaler). 1952.

Fisher, Nancy. "Fantasy and Reality in the Poetry of Randall Jarrell," (Drake). 1969.

Fowler, Elizabeth (Thomas). "Annotated Edition of the Letters of Vachel Lindsay to Nellie Vieira," (F. D. Miller). 1968.

Frederick, Joan. "Variations Upon a Theme: The Use of Physical Disabilities in Melville's Fiction," (Wright). 1973.

Friman, Anne Elizabeth. "A Critical Survey of Helen Waddell's Medieval Studies," (Stockton). 1964.

Fykes, Beverly Jean. "The Fairest Hope of Heaven: Love and Marriage in Hawthorne's Works," (Wright). 1974.

Garloch, Gail. "Role-Playing and the Idea of the Play in Ben Jonson's Comedies," (Sanders). 1975.

Garner, Frances Adrian. "Henry James's Use of Architecture," (Wright). 1974.

Gasque, Alice T. "The Idea of the Poet in the Works of William Dunbar," (Fisher). 1974.

Gasque, Thomas James, "A Study of Some Ritual Aspects of Old English Poetry," (Isaacs). 1970.

Gibson, Phillip J. "A State Mirror of Richard II : Shakespeare's Play as Produced at Stratford-upon-Avon," (Sanders). 1986.

Glickfield, Charlotte Woods. "Some Underlying Themes in The Waverley Novels," (Curry). 1967.

Gordon, Douglas Kirke. "The Thomas Hughes Free Public Library, Rugby, Tennessee: A History and Partial Bibliography," (Curry). 1974.

Graham, Jean Bettis. "'This World's Stage': Reality, Illusion, and the Play-Within-A-Play in the Dramatic Works of John Marston," (Sanders). 1981.

Gribble, Barbara. "To Grow to Be a Hero: The Influence of Thomas Carlyle, upon the Late Prose Romances of William Morris," (Kelly). 1981.

Gwin, Minrose, C. "The Peculiar Sisterhood: Black and White Women of the Old South in American Literature," (Shurr). 1983.

Hait, Elizabeth A. "The City of Paris; A Shape and A Shaping Force in Selected Nineteenth-Century British Fiction," (Kelly). 1985.

Haluska, Jan C. "Master and Slave in the First Four Novels of J.M. Coetzee," (Penner) 1987.

Hambright, David Arnold. "The Vices and Virtues in the Evolution of the Grotesque from Medieval to Modern Literature," (Fisher). 1977.

Hamm, Robert Wayne. "An Analysis of the Confisyon del Amante, the Castilian Translation of Gower's Confessio Amantis," (Fisher). 1975.

Hardwig, Marilyn Ross. "Henry James's American Males in Europe: Roderick Hudson, The American, The Ambassadors, and The Golden Bowl." (Wright). 1978.

Harkey, Joseph Harry. "Don Quixote and American Fiction through Mark Twain, " (Davis). 1967.

Hauer, Stanley Richard. "A Commentary on the Old English Exodus," (Richards). 1978.

Hecht, Harvey Edgar. "The Use and Development of the Narrators in the Short Fiction of Edgar Allan Poe," (Davis). 1972.

Herrin, Roberta R. "H. L. Mencken as a Philologist," (Fisher). 1986.

Higgs, Robert Jackson. "The Unheroic Hero: A Study of the Athlete in Twentieth-Century American Literature," (Davis). 1967.

Hilenski, Ferdinand A., II. "The Emblem of Print: Manifestations of an Aesthetic of Print in the Spectator," (Adams). 1974.

Hilton, Chadwick Buford. "An Edition and Study of the Old English Seasons for Fasting," (Richards). 1984.

Hodge, Marion Cecil, Jr. "What Moment Is Not Terrible?: An Introduction to the Work of Joyce Carol Oates," (Penner). 1974.

Hogue, Louis Lynn. "An Edition of 'Eight Charges delivered,

at so many several General Sessions, & Gaol Deliveries:
Held at Charles Town. . . . In the Years 1703. 1704.
1705. 1706. 1707 . . . . By Nicholas Trott Esq; Chief
Justice of the Province of South Carolina', (Davis).
1972.

Hollingsworth, Helen. "A Kindle of Hybrids: A Study of
Narrative Techniques in the Romance and Tale of the
Early Seventeenth Century," (Sanders). 1971.

Hood, Mary Connie Kelly. "A Search for Authority:
Prolegomena to a Definitive Critical Edition of W. B.
Yeats's A Vision," (Sanders). 1983.

Hudnall, Michael Benjamin. "Moral Design in the Plays of
Sir Charles Sedley," (Armistead). 1984.

Hughes, Susan Eileen Streett. "English in the Letter-Books
and Plea and Memoranda Rolls of the Corporation of
London, 1377-1422, in Comparison with Contemporaneous
Chancery English: Their Possible Roles in the Evolution
of Chancery Standard and Modern English," (Fisher).
1978.

Hungiville, Maurice Neill. "Rudyard Kipling's Reputation as
a Poet, 1886-1969," (Knickerbocker). 1969.

James, Katherine Harriett. "The Widow in Jacobean Drama,"
(Sanders). 1973.

Jenkins, William Warren. "Three Centuries in the
Development of the Pocahontas Story in American
Literature," (Davis).
1977.

Jenks, Mary Hathaway. "Literary Criticism in the Quarterly
Review, 1809-1824," (Curry). 1957.

Jones, Mabel Jean. "The Regional English of the Former
Inhabitants of Cades Cove in the Great Smoky Mountains,"
(Orton). 1973.

Kalinevitch, Karen. "Ralph Waldo Emerson's Older Brother: The Letters and Journal of William Emerson," (Ensor). 1982.

Kay, Carol Ruth McGinnis. "'Such Factious Emulations:' Dramatic Imagery in Shakespeare's Henry VI Trilogy," (Sanders). 1967.

Kay, Wayne Donald. "'After Smoke the Light': The Short Story in the Spectator, (Lyles). 1967.

Keenan, Hugh Thomas. "The Apocalyptic Vision in Old English Poetry," (Isaacs). 1968.

Kearney, Martin F. "Pollyanalytics and Spirit of Place in D. H. Lawrence's Short Fiction," (Schneider). 1984.

Kelly, Mary Quella. "An Approach to an Old English Poetics," (Isaacs). 1969.

Kelly, Michael. "The Trial Scenes in the Plays of the Beaumont and Fletcher Folio," (Sanders). 1966.

Kemp, Homer Dale. "The Pre-Revolutionary Virginia Polemical Essay: The Pistol Fee and the Two-Penny Acts Controversies," (Davis). 1972.

Kemper, Kristie Ann. "The Search for a Political Theory in the Fiction of Herman Melville," (Wright). 1975.

Kennedy, Evelyn S. "The Wasteland Worlds of Augustus and Victoria. (R. M. Kelly). 1988.

Kennedy, Sally Pitts (Slocum). "Vestiges of Rule Ritual in Sir Gawain and the Green Knight," (Isaacs). 1968.

Killingsworth, Myrth Jimmie. "Whitman's Sexual Themes: A Historical Approach," (F. D. Miller). 1979.

Killman, Robin R. "Reflections of the Pleiade Aesthetic in Edmund Spenser's Minor Poems," (Stewart). 1985.

Kinney, James Joseph. "The Theme of Miscegenation in the American Novel to World War I," (F. D. Miller). 1972.

Kirkland, James Wilton. "Animal Imagery in the Fiction of Herman Melville," (Wright). 1969.

Knowles, Jack L. "Thomas d"Urfey's Adaptations of Renaissance Plays," (Armistead). 1984.

Krause, Florence (Phyfer). "The Grammatical Aspect of Browning's Style," (Knickerbocker). 1970.

Lackey, Allen Doyle. "Flannery O'Connor and Her Critics: A Survey and Evaluation of the Critical Response to the Fiction of Flannery O'Connor," (Drake). 1972.

Lanier, Rene Parks, Jr. "Aspects of Sublimity in the Poetry of Lord Byron," (Curry). 1972.

Lasater, Alice Elizabeth. "Hispano-Arabic Relationships to the Works of the Gawain-Poet," (Isaacs). 1971.

Lawrence, Bonnie Lew (Strother).. "The Imagery in the Sermons of Thomas Shephard," (Davis). 1968.

Leazer, Susan Adkin. "Spenserian Comedy: The Faerie Queene, Books III and IV," (Stewart). 1977.

Lee, Ernest D. "The Grotesque in the Poetry of William Wordsworth," (Bratton). 1986.

Lee, Gordon K. "The Roles of Women in the Apocalyptic Myths of Coleridge and Keats," (N. Goslee). 1987.

Levy, Robert Allen. "Dryden's Translation of Chaucer: A Study of the Means of Re-creating Literary Models," (Adams). 1973.

Lewis, Mineko S. "Humor Characterization in Restoration Comedy," (Adams). 1973.

Lewter, John Neams. "John Locke and The Spectator: Aspects of Virtue," (Adams). 1974.

Litzinger, Boyd Anthony. "Robert Browning's Reputation as a Thinker, 1889-1955," (Knickerbocker). 1956.

Lyday-Lee, Kathy. "Selected Mountain Literature of Will Allen Dromgoole," (Ensor). 1982.

Mathews, James W. "Hawthorne and Howells: The Middle Way in American Fiction," (Wright). 1960.

McAleer, Edward C. "Letters of Browning to Isabella Blagden: An Edition," (Knickerbocker). 1950.

McBride, Bailey B. "The Poetry of James Thomson (1700-1748)," (Adams). 1966.

McClelland, Charles Blake. "A Critical Edition of William Congreve's Love for Love," (Lyles). 1970.

McCrory, J. V. "A Study of Robert Browning's Representative Personal Satires," (Knickerbocker). 1967.

McKinstry, Douglas. "Mark Twain's Mississippi River Geniuses," (Ensor). 1987.

McManus, Eva B. "The Growth Toward Mature Love in four of Shakespeare's Comedies and Romances," (N. Sanders). 1988

McMath, Martha Whitney Vickers. "Feminine Identity in Anais Nin's Cities of the Interior," (Penner). 1978.

Martin, Larry Alan. "Out of the Solitary Chamber: The Politics of Nathaniel Hawthorne," (Ensor). 1980.

Mason, James David. "Monsters with Human Voices: The Anthropomorphic Adversary of the Hero in Old Norse and Old English Literature," (Kratz). 1976.

Matchen, David Elba. "Prophet, Preacher, Mountebank: Defoe and His Methods of Persuasion in the Review," (Adams). 1976.

Mayberry, Susan Neal. "The Adulterous Wife in Renaissance Drama," (Sanders). 1982.

Maynor, Natalie. "Joseph Beaumont's Psyche in the Seventeenth-Century Context," (Wheeler). 1978.

Merrill, Harry George, III. "Milton's Secret Adversary" Peter Du Moulin and the Politics of Protestant Humanism," (Lievsay). 1959.

Miller, Tracey Russell. "An Investigation of the Regional English of Unicoi County, Tennessee" (Orton). 1973.

Millsaps, Ellen McNutt. "The Family in Four Novels of Eudora Welty." (Drake). 1976.

Mobley, Janice Edens. "Eating, Drinking, and Smoking in Melville's Fiction," (Wright). 1974.

Mobley, Lawrence Frank. "Time in the Painting and Poetry of Dante Gabriel Rossetti," (Kelly). 1974.

Modlin, Charles Ernest. "Political Satire in America, 1789-1801," (F. D. Miller). 1969.

Moehlmann, John Frederick. "A Concordance to the Poetry of John Wilmot, Earl of Rochester, With an Introductory Essay on His Use of Language," (Adams). 1974.

Moran, William Charles. "Tennyson's Reputation as a Thinker," (Knickerbocker). 1965.

Morgan, William Woodrow, Jr. "Thomas Hardy's Reputation as a Poet," (Knickerbocker). 1969.

Morlier, Margaret M. "Elizabeth Barrett Browning's Poetics of Passion," (N.M. Goslee). 1986.

Morrell, Minnie Cate. "A Manual of Old English Biblical Materials," (Parker). 1952.

Morris, Douglas Kelly. "Noctes Ambrosianae: The Influence of Blackwood's Magazine," (Curry). 1972.

Morris, John William. "Thomas Carlyle's Influence on George Meredith's Theory of Literature," (Knickerbocker). 1954.

Morton, Gerald W. "A Critical Edition of Mildmay Fane's De Pugna Animi," (Sanders). 1984.

Moses, Anthony K. "The Legend of Morte de Arthur," (Richards). 1983.

Murray, Barbara Marie. The Scarlet Experiment: Emily Dickinson's Abortion Experience. (Shurr). 1988.

Nakhai, Mandana. "The Safar Namih (Travel Journal) of the Persian Nasir Khusrau (A.D. 1003-1072). Translated into English With an Introduction and Notes," (Adams). 1979.

Neel, Jasper Phillip. "'A Kind of Mungrel Breed': The Allusive Method in Butler's Hudibras.'" (Adams). 1975.

Nelson, Emmanuel Sampath. "Alienated Rebels: John Rechy and James Baldwin," (Schneider). 1983.

Norman, Rose Lynn. "Autobiographies of American Women Writers to 1914," (Wright). 1979.

Novak, Frank G., Jr. "Lewis Mumford as a Critic of American Culture" (Wright). 1975.

Null, Linda. "James Boswell's Concept of Liberty in the Era of the American Revolution," (Adams). 1977.

Palmer, Joyce Cornette, "Boswell's Life of Johnson as Literary History," (Lyles). 1967.

Palmer, Leslie Howard. "The Ironic Mr. Hardy: Irony as a Technique in the Novels of Thomas Hardy," (Knickerbocker). 1966.

Parker, John Howard. "The Life and Works of James Howell Street," (Ensor). 1978.

Parrill, Anna Sue. "The Theme of Revolution in the English Novel from Disraeli to Conrad," (Knickerbocker). 1965.

Parrill, William Bruce. "The Elizabethan Conception of Hell, the Devil, the Magician, and the Witch, and their Use in Elizabethan Fiction," (Stewart). 1964.

Patton, Doris. The Physeter and the Great White Whale: The Influence of Rabelais on Moby Dick. (Shurr). 1988.

Pemberton, James Michael. "'An Inward and Spiritual Grace': The Southern Gentleman of the Antebellum Novel," (Davis). 1973.

Perkins, James Ashbrook. "An American Rhapsody: The Poetry of Kenneth Fearing," (Leggett). 1972.

Phillips, Elizabeth (Crow). "The Literary Life of John Tomlin, Friend of Poe," (Davis). 1953.

Powers, Katherine Richardson. "The Influence of William Godwin on the Novels of Mary Shelley," (Curry). 1972.

Price, Joseph Elmer, Jr. "Some Aspects of the Gnomic Elements in Anglo-Saxon Poetry," (Stockton). 1967.

Purvis, Tomsye Dale. "A Study of Spenser's Fowre Hymnes," (Stewart). 1976.

Pyrek, Carolyn Morris. "The Contemplative, Narrative, and Dramatic Modes in the Poetry of Thomas Hardy," (Leggett). 1975.

Pyrek, Steven Joseph. "Thomas Shadwell's Comedies: The Evolution of Conscious Artistry," (Adams). 1976.

Railsback, Jo Helen. "The Thomas Becket Story as a Theme in Dramatic Literature," (Knickerbocker). 1969.

Rees, Charles A. "Lady Bright and Her Children: Contemporary American Gay Drama," (Burghardt). 1988.

Reese, James Robert. "Variation in Appalachian English: A Study of the Speech of Elderly, Rural Natives of East Tennessee," (Dumas). 1977.

Reeves, Pamela. "Hawthorne's Settings: Forest, City, Country, and Garden," (Wright). 1974.

Reilly, Rosalind Brock. "The Scarlet Letter and the Art of Reading," (Kelly). 1983.

Relihan, Mary Patricia. "The Language of the English Stonor Letters, 1420-1483," (Fisher). 1977.

Rich, Julia Ann. "Thomas Southerne, Restoration Playwright," (Adams). 1979.

Richards, Michael Reynard. "The Romantic Critics' Opinions of Elizabethan Non-Dramatic Literature," (Stewart). 1972.

Richardson, Malcolm, II. "The Influence of Henry V on the Development of Chancery English," (Fisher). 1978.

Robey, Cora. "Mathew Arnold's Concept of Culture on the Late Victorian Novel: The Operation of this Idea in the Novels of George Eliot, George Meredith, Thomas Hardy, and George Gissing," (Knickerbocker). 1966.

Ruf, Barbara Butler. "John Davis: Poet, Novelist, and Traveler," (Davis). 1974.

Schaible, Robert Manly. "An Annotated Edition of Herman Melville's Redburn," (Wright). 1971.

Scruton, James A. "A Vocable Ground: The Poetry of Seamus Heaney. (Leggett). 1988.

Sekula, Jeffrey Charles. "The Role of Romanticism in Stephen Spender's Criticism and Poetry: A Study in Artistic Vision," (Leggett). 1972.

Shields, John Charles. "Phillis Wheatley's Poetics of Ascent," (R. B. Miller). 1978.

Shonk, Timothy Allen. "A Study of the Auchinleck Manuscript: Investigations into the Processes of Book Making in the Fourteenth Century," (Fisher). 1981.

Skinner, Mary Lynn. "The Interpolated Story in Selected Novels of Fielding and Smollett," (Lyles). 1968.

Small, Julianne. "Classical Allusions in the Fiction of Herman Melville," (Wright). 1974.

Spornick, Nickolas Byron. "The Satire in the Novels of Thomas Love Peacock," (Curry). 1969.

Spurgeon, Patrick O'Dyer. "The Poet Historical: Edmund Spenser. A Study of Renaissance Methods and Uses of History," (Stewart). 1963.

Stanfield, Jane S. "Standardization in Anglo-Saxon Laws: A Diplomatic Study," (Fisher). 1984.

Stargardt, Ute. "The Influence of Dorothea von Montau on the Mysticism of Margery Kempe," (Fisher). 1981.

Stedman, Stephen J. "Unifying Motifs in the Plays of John Banks with Special Attention to the Imagery," (Armistead). 1982.

Storey, Kenneth Ervin. "Shadow and Substance: The Management of Tone in Tennyson's The Princess," (Knickerbocker). 1967.

Surrency, Jack Edward. "The Kentucky Tragedy in American Literature: From Thomas Holley Chivers to Robert Penn Warren," (Davis). 1977.

Sutton, John C. "Hegelian Synthesis in the Works of Nathaniel Hawthorne," (Shurr). 1986.

Tanenbaum, Miles B. "Walt Whitman and American Art," (Shurr). 1988.

Templeton, Barbara A. "A Feminist Theory of Poetics," (Leggett). 1984.

Thomas, James Walter. "Lyle Saxon: A Critical Introduction to the Man and His Works," (Ensor). 1975.

Tierce, Michael T. "Eggs, Small Beer, and Hardy: The Poetry and Prose of Philip Larkin," (Leggett). 1985.

True, Warren Roberts. "Chekhovian Dramaturgy in the Plays of Tennessee Williams, Harold Pinter, and Ed Bullines," (Burghardt). 1976.

Varner, Jeanine Baker. "Henry James and Gustave Flaubert: Their Creative Relationship," (Adams). 1981.

Varner, Paul Stanley. "The Comic Techniques of George Colman the Elder," (Adams). 1981.

von Brentano, Alisa R. "Marlowe and Melville," (Sanders and Wright). 1985.

Wages, Jack Douglas. "Southern Colonial Elegiac Verse," (Davis). 1968.

Walter, Donna. "Twentieth-Century Woman in the Early Novels of Doris Lessing," (Penner). 1978.

Ward, Carol Marie. "Movie as Metaphor in Contemporary Fiction: A Study of Walker Percy, Larry McMurtry, and John Fowles," (Leggett). 1981.

Ward, Wilber Henry, III. "Bacon's Rebellion in Literature to 1861," (Davis). 1971.

Ware, Malcolm Roney. "Sublimity in the Major British Novelists of the Eighteenth and Early Nineteenth Centuries: A Study of Contemporary Taste Reflected in the Novel of the Period," (Curry). 1959.

Warren, John W. "Walter Savage Landor's Views on English Life and Literature: A Critical Study of His English Imaginary Conversations," (Curry). 1961.

Weathersby, Robert Warren, II. "Joseph Holt Ingraham: A Critical Introduction to the Man and His Works," (Davis). 1974.

Weinkauf, Mary (Stanley). "The Two Faces of Eve: The Ideal and the Bad Renaissance Wife in Paradise Lost," (Wheeler).

White, Leslie T. "Uproar in the Echo: Robert Browning's Poetry of Vitalism," (Kelly). 1984.

White, Rita Sizemore. "The Prosody of Michael Drayton's Pastorals," (Stewart). 1971.

Wiggins, Genevieve Elizabeth. "The Brownings and Napoleon III: A Study in Political Poetry," (Kelly). 1973.

Wilson, B. J. "Deception in the Comedies and Tragicomedies of John Fletcher," (Sanders). 1987.

Wilson, Herman Pledger. "Chaucer as a Prose Writer," (Parker). 1956.

Woodall, Guy Ramon. "Robert Walsh, Jr., as an Editor and Literary Critic: 1797-1836," (Davis). 1966.

Woodard, Charles R. "Browning and Three Modern Poets: Pound, Yeats, and Eliot," (Daniel and Knickerbocker). 1953.

Woods, James Sabord. "Swift's Sermons: Their Backgrounds, Their Rhetoric, and Their Relationships to the Total Canon," (Adams). 1975.

Woolley, Andrew Price. "God of Law, God of Grace: the Concept of God in Edmund Spenser's The Faerie Queene," (Stewart). 1978.

Wooten, Elizabeth Harper. "Biblical Allusion in the Novels of Richardson," (Adams). 1973.

Young, Eugene Owen. "Keepers of the Faith: Sports from the Wilderness to the Space Age in Selected Modern American Novels," (Leggett). 1979.

Zimmerman, Elena Irish. "American Opera Librettos, 1767-1825: The Manifestation and Result of the Imitative Principle in an American Literary Form," (Davis). 1973.

Zion, Rhoda Piner. "Sublimity and Effect in the Short Fiction of Edgar Allan Poe," (Davis). 1973.